The Kids'

World Almanac®

of Amazing Facts

about Numbers,

Math, and Money

Also by Margery Facklam

Who Harnessed the Horse?
Healing Drugs (with Howard Facklam)
Bees Dance and Whales Sing
I Eat Dinner
I Go to Sleep
And Then There Was One
Partners for Life
Do Not Disturb
The Trouble with Mothers
Avalanche! (with Howard Facklam)
Plants—Survival or Extinction (with Howard Facklam)
Spare Parts for People (with Howard Facklam)
Changes in the Wind (with Howard Facklam)
So Can I
But Not Like Mine
The Brain (with Howard Facklam)
From Cell to Clone (with Howard Facklam)

Also by Margaret Thomas

Volcano!

The Kids'

World Almanac®

MARGERY FACKLAM and

# of Amazing Facts

MARGARET THOMAS

about Numbers,

Illustrated by Paul Facklam

Math, and Money

WORLD ALMANAC

AN IMPRINT OF PHAROS BOOKS · A SCRIPPS HOWARD COMPANY

NEW YORK

First published in 1992.

Library of Congress Cataloging-in-Publication Data
Facklam, Margery.
Kids' world almanac of amazing facts about numbers, math, and money / by Margery Facklam and Margaret Thomas.
p.   cm.
Includes bibliographical references and index.
Summary: Examines the importance and meaning of numbers and how they are used in such areas as weights and measures, money, and signs and symbols.
ISBN 0-88687-635-4. — ISBN 0-88687-634-6 (pbk.)
1. Counting—Juvenile literature.   2. Number concept—Juvenile literature.   3. Money—Juvenile literature.   [1. Number concept.   2. Counting.]   I. Thomas, Margaret.   II. Title.
QA113.F33   1992
513—dc20   92-6679
CIP
AC

Printed in the United States of America
Pharos Books are available at special discounts on bulk purchases for sales promotions, premiums, fundraising, or educational use. For details, contact the Special Sales Department, Pharos Books, 200 Park Avenue, New York, NY 10166.

Jacket design by Charles Kreloff
Jacket illustration by Mark Teague
Interior design by Laura Hough

Pharos Books
A Scripps Howard Company
200 Park Avenue
New York, NY 10166

10   9   8   7   6   5   4   3   2   1

For Howard Facklam and Fran Thomas,

two terrific husbands,

who helped us with

our math.

Contents

CONTENTS

Acknowledgments

We thank Jeffery Facklam from Streamwood, Illinois, and Christopher Facklam from Tonawanda, New York, who helped us find number riddles. We are especially glad that Mrs. Wohlever, a math teacher at Oakhill Elementary School in Streamwood, Illinois, showed Jeff Facklam a good way to remember how to multiply by nines, so that he could teach his grandma how to do it, at last!

We also appreciate the help of the writer's best friends—librarians, especially Pegg Skotnicki at the Buffalo and Erie County Public Library; the staff and volunteers at the Clarence, New York, library; and the Baseball Hall of Fame Library in Cooperstown, New York.

Just

CHAPTER ONE

Numbers

WHO THOUGHT UP NUMBERS?

Imagine a caveman in the Stone Age trying to keep track of all the members of the clan before there were numbers for counting. He might have used small stones, one for each person. If he matched a pebble to a person, he'd know that no one was missing, but he still wouldn't know how many people lived in that group. Numbers tell us "how many." The word *calculate* comes from the Latin word *calculus*, which means pebble or small stone. Even now there are some groups of people who do not have a counting system. In the state of Mato Grosso in Brazil, at the edge of the Amazon jungle, the Nambiquara Indians have no numbers. They have only one word, a verb that means "to be two alike."

For a long time people used a *tally* system, making one mark for each object. A hunter might make a notch in a stick for each deer he had killed. Or he might draw marks in the dirt for each day that had passed since a full moon.

Next, someone figured out how to put the tally marks in groups of five. But gradually, as those early people developed a language, they found words to use in place of pebbles or tally marks. The counting words were a big step because the last word used named the total number of things being counted: one, two, three, four, five, and so on. And next came symbols for the counting words. The symbols are called *numerals*. The numerals 1 to 9 are also called *digits*. Our fingers are called digits, too. No surprise, since people counted on their fingers even before they made tally marks. Our base 10 is based on the ancient ten-finger counting. The Mayans of Central America used a base 20. Maybe they counted both fingers and toes.

"The end is bent," said the people in one tribe of Native Americans for the number 1. This referred to the practice of bending the little finger to indicate 1. "It is bent once more" meant the number 2. The number 3 was a word meaning "The middle is bent," and 4 was "Only one remains." All the fingers bent for 5 was "My hand is finished."

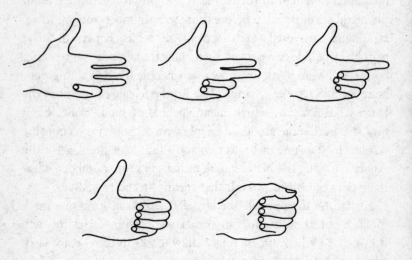

Clues that tell us how numbers are named are hidden in many languages. In the Russian language, *pyat* means five, and *pyad* means "hand with five fingers spread out." The Persian word for five is *pantcha*, and the word for hand is *pentcha*. The number eleven comes from an Old English word *endleofan*, which means "ten and one left over." Twelve comes from the Old English word *twelf* that means "two left."

But No Zero

The zero has been called one of the most important inventions of arithmetic. The ancient Egyptians used a zero just to separate two numbers, but they never put the zero at the end of a number. For example, they didn't add a zero to one to make 10, or two zeros to make 100. Instead, 10 had its own symbol, and 100 had another.

The Chinese didn't have a symbol for zero either, but they did have a position on their abacus, or counting beads, that meant "nothing."

The Mayans in South America also discovered the zero.

It was the Hindu astronomers of India who discovered the amazing zero. The Hindu word for emptiness was *sunya*. It was used to mean an empty place in a number, such as 105. But centuries passed before mathematicians decided that sunya, the empty space, was actually a useful number, the "nothing" number, a zero. The zero in 105 means that there is a 1 in the hundreds place, nothing in the tens place, and a 5 in the ones place.

Another 800 years went by before anyone else heard of the wonderful zero that made it possible to add, subtract, multiply, or divide numbers accurately. The zero became a decimal place number.

ANCIENT NUMBER SYSTEMS

Numerals have been found on ancient stone tablets, on temple walls, and on scrolls of papyrus. Here are some of them:

Egyptian:

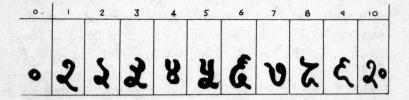

Hindu-Arabic:

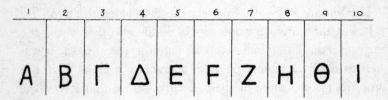

Ancient Greek (Ionic):

1	2	3	4	5	6	7	8	9	10
A	B	Γ	Δ	E	F	Z	H	θ	I

Babylonian:

Hebrew:

1	2	3	4	5	6	7	8	9	10
א	ב	ג	ד	ה	ו	ז	ח	ט	י

Chinese:

一 二 三 四 五 六 七 八 九 十 百 千
1   2   3   4   5   6   7   8   9   10   100   1,000

MAYAN: The Mayans used combinations of three symbols for writing all the numbers in their base 20 system: a dot, a line, and a decorated oval.

1	2	3	4	5	6	7	8	9	10

20	40	60	80	100	120	140	160	180	200

ARABIC NUMBERS

The Arabs adopted the earlier Hindu system of numbers and made it their own. That system spread to Europe during the 1200s, and that's what we use today, Arabic numbers.

1	2	3	4	5	6	7	8	9		1,000 years ago
1	2	3	4	5	6	7	8	9	0	800 years ago
1	2	3	4	5	6	7	8	9	0	600 years ago
1	2	3	4	5	6	7	8	9	10	Today

ROMAN NUMERALS

The Romans invented a system of counting we still call Roman numerals. At first their numerals were scratches in sand or clay. One scratch was 1, two scratches were 2, and so on. For 10, they made an X. A 5 was a V, the top half the ten's X. But they had no zero, so they had no way to multiply or divide their numbers. Roman numerals were only good for keeping records, and knowing "how many." We still find Roman numerals on old buildings, on clocks, to number chapters in books, or on outlines. Until the 1500s, people used Roman numerals for everyday math.

I = 1   C = 100
V = 5   D = 500
X = 10   M = 1,000
L = 50

- To read a number in Roman numerals, you just add up the numerals from left to right, adding large numbers to the smaller ones like this: VI = 6 (V = 5 and I = 1, so 5 + 1 = 6).
- When the first number is the smaller one, you subtract it from the larger number like this: IV = 4 (I taken away from V = IV, or 1 taken away from 5 = 4).
- A line over the top of a Roman numeral multiplies its value by 1,000. For example: V = 5, but $\overline{V} = 5 \times 1,000 = 5,000$.

Roman numerals	Arabic numerals
III	1 + 1 + 1 = 3
VIII (V + III)	8 = 5 + 3
XXVIII (XX + V + III)	28 = 20 + 5 + 3
IX (X − I)	9
XL (L − X)	50 − 10 = 40
MCDXCII (M + (D − C) + (C − X) + II)	1 + 400 + 90 + 2 = 1492

Can you figure out these dates?
MDCCLXXVI (1776)
MMX (2010)

WHY DO ASTRONAUTS COUNT DOWN?

The idea of counting "10, 9, 8, 7, 6, 5, 4, 3, 2, 1 Lift off!" started long before we even had any rockets or space ships. It was invented by a German movie maker in 1928 for a science fiction film called *The Girl in the Moon*. He wanted to make the scene more exciting than just "1, 2, 3, Go," and it was. The fake movie rocket blasted off in a puff of smoke and movie-goers loved it. When scientists built real rockets, they discovered that the countdown was a good way of checking off last-minute details.

HANDY HELPER

In ancient times, everyone counted on their fingers, but now we're not supposed to. On the other hand, it's nice to have a little help, especially if you have trouble remembering how to multiply by 9. Try this—it works!

Step 1: Hold your hands out in front of you, palms down. Imagine that each finger is numbered, starting with 1 on the little finger of your left hand, like this:

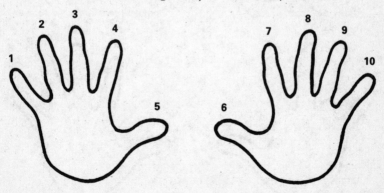

Step 2: Fold down the finger number 1.

Step 3: If you count the number of fingers standing to the left of finger 1, you'll find none. Then count the number of fingers standing to the right of finger one, and you'll find nine. The answer to 1 × 9 is 9. Of course, that's a simple one.

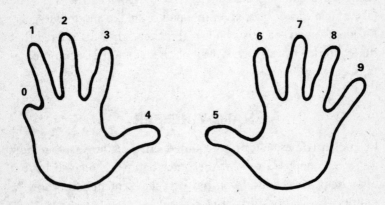

- Try 2 × 9. Put down the finger numbered 2. Count the fingers standing to the left, and you'll find one. Now count the fingers to the right, to get eight. The answer to 2 × 9 is 18.

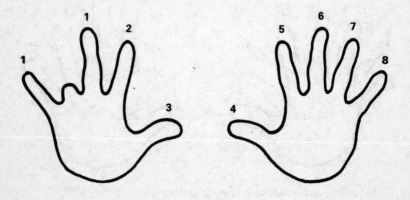

- Or 3 × 9. Put down the finger numbered 3. Count the fingers standing to the left, and you'll find two. The fingers standing to the right are seven 3 × 9 = 27.

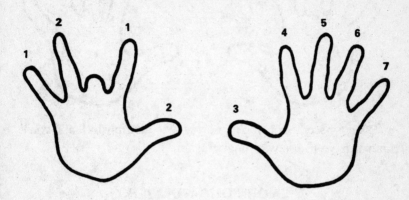

- How about 6 × 9? The number 6 finger is down. How many fingers stand to the left? How many stand to the right? Did you get 54? 6 × 9 = 54.

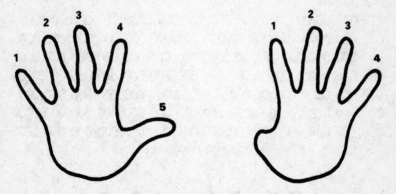

- Try 9 × 9: When finger number 9 is down, how many fingers are standing to the left? (Eight). How many are standing to the right? (One). So the answer is 9 × 9 = ——.

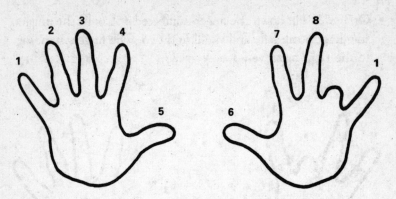

Don't worry. Soon you'll know how to multiply by 9 and you'll never have to use your fingers again.

ENORMOUS NUMBERS

The word *million* has been in the English language since 1370, and the word *trillion* since 1480. The highest number in the United States is the *centillion*, which is 1 followed by 303 zeros, like this:

1,000,000,000,000,000,000,000,000,000,000,000,
000,000,000,000,000,000,000,000,000,000,000,000,000,
000,000,000,000,000,000,000,000,000,000,000,000,000,
000,000,000,000,000,000,000,000,000,000,000,000,000,
000,000,000,000,000,000,000,000,000,000,000,000,000,
000,000,000,000,000,000,000,000,000,000,000,000,000,
000,000,000,000,000,000,000,000,000,000,000,000,000,
000,000,000,000.

Making Big Numbers Small

Instead of writing out huge numbers like a centillion, mathematicians invented **exponents**. An exponent is a little number written above the base number that tells you how many times to multiply the base number by itself. A centillion is written as 10^{303}. It tells you to multiply 10×10 303 times. When the base number is 10, it's easy because the exponent tells you how many zeros to write down—in this case 303.

How Many Zeros?

Billion has 9 zeros

Trillion has 12 zeros

Quadrillion has 15 zeros

Quintillion has 18 zeros

Sextillion has 21 zeros

Septillion has 24 zeros

Octillion has 27 zeros

Nonillion has 30 zeros

Decillion has 33 zeros

Undecillion has 36 zeros

Duodecillion has 39 zeros

Tredecillion has 42 zeros

Quattuordecillion has 45 zeros

Quindecillion has 48 zeros

Sexdecillion has 51 zeros

Septendecillion has 54 zeros

Octodecillion has 57 zeros

Novemdecillion has 60 zeros

Vigintillion has 63 zeros

Googol has 100 zeros

Googolplex has a googol of zeros.

WHO THOUGHT UP A GOOGOL?

Edward Kasner was born in New York City in 1878. He was only eight years old when he solved a very difficult math problem and his teacher told him he'd be a great mathematician. And he was. When he was working with numbers that had hundreds of zeros, he asked his two nephews to make up a name for them. The two boys invented the words *googol* and *googolplex*.

Infinity

Infinity was invented by mathematicians to mean that numbers can go on forever without end. There is no largest number. You can always count another and another. But there cannot be an infinity of real things, such as stones or grains of sand. It applies only to numbers. The symbol for infinity is:

What Is the Largest Number That Can Be Written with Three Digits?

9×9^9, which means that 9 is raised to its 387,420,489th power. Written out, the row of digits for this number would be about 600 miles long and take 150 years to read.

PERFECT NUMBERS

"Perfect" is the name given to a number that is the sum of its factors. For example, 6 is a perfect number because it's made up of the factors 1, 2, and 3, and they add up to 6: $1 + 2 + 3 = 6$. Other perfect numbers are 28, 496, and 8,128. Two thousand years ago, when a Greek mathematician found them, he thought these numbers were so rare that he called them perfect.

PRIME NUMBERS

A prime number is one that has no factors but 1 itself. In other words, it can't be divided evenly by any other number. Some prime numbers are 3, 5, 7, 11, and 13.

ODD NUMBERS

A number is odd when it can be divided by two, leaving a remainder of 1. Odd numbers are 1, 3, 5, 7, 9, 11, 13, and so on.

EVEN NUMBERS

An even number is one that has no remainder—nothing left over—when divided by 2, such as 2, 4, 6, 8, 200, 242.

NEGATIVE NUMBERS

A negative number has a minus sign in front of it because it is less than zero. How can anything be smaller than zero? And why would we need negative numbers? If you had $5.00, for example, and spent all of it on comic books and candy, you'd have $0.00. If you borrowed $2.00 from a friend, then you'd have −$2.00, a negative number, because you owed that amount.

WHAT IS AVERAGE?

Has anyone ever told you that you are above average height, or below average weight? What did they mean? Suppose your mom's driving you and six other neighborhood kids to school. One kid is five years old, one is six, one is fourteen, one is thirteen, two are ten, and you are twelve. What's the average age of the kids in the van?

To find out, you add up all the ages: $5 + 6 + 14 + 13 + 10 + 10 + 12 = 70$.

Next, divide that sum by the number of kids: 70 divided by 7 = 10.

The average age is ten. You, at age twelve, and two other kids are above the average age in the car. Two kids are average, and two are below the average age.

WHAT'S THE DIFFERENCE BETWEEN ARITHMETIC AND MATHEMATICS?

Mathematics is the science that studies and explains numbers, quantities, measurements, shapes, patterns, and how all these things are related. Arithmetic is the computational part of mathematics that includes adding, subtracting, multiplying, and dividing numbers.

MACHINES THAT HELP US COUNT

Abacus

Other than fingers, the abacus is the oldest known counting gadget. It was first used in Central Asia. The Chinese people call it *suan pan*, the Japanese people call it a *soroban*, and the Russians call it *s'choty*.

The abacus is a frame with nine rows of beads that slide on wire. It is simple, fast, and it doesn't need batteries. The beads are separated by a crossbar. The two horizontal rows on top are called the "heaven" beads, and the five rows on the bottom are the "earth" beads. Each heaven bead has a value of 5. Each earth bead has a value of 1. To show a number on an abacus, you push the beads toward the crossbar. Starting from the right, the first vertical row of beads stands for the ones, the next for the tens, the next for the hundreds, and so on.

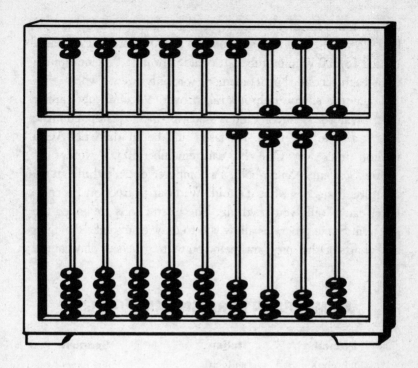

Calculator

The first calculator was invented in 1642 by Blaise Pascal. It could only add and subtract. In 1671, Gottfried Wilhelm Leibniz invented the first calculator that could multiply and divide.

Computers

A computer is a machine for storing and processing information. It takes any information typed in and changes it into a *binary code*, which is a code made up of only zeros and ones. The zero and one signals turn electric switches on and off.

The first computer was built in 1946. It was called ENIAC,

which stands for Electronic Numeral Integrator and Computer. ENIAC weighed 50 tons and took up 2,000 square feet of space. It used 18,000 vacuum tubes. It could perform 3,000 multiplications each second, but its memory was only twenty words.

Today the **silicon chip** has taken over. Vacuum tubes aren't used anymore. A silicon chip is a quarter-inch square, about the size of a little fingernail. It's faster and better than ENIAC a million times over. One chip can remember 50,000 words.

Are Computers Smart? No. A computer doesn't think; it's a machine that does what it's told. Without instructions, a computer can't "tell" you anything. The instructions are called the *program*. Some programs allow you to draw or to make diagrams and charts. Other programs help you write papers or play games.

NUMBERS IN FOREIGN LANGUAGES

	French	Italian	Spanish
1	un (uhn)	un (oon)	uno (oo-noh)
2	deux (duh)	due (dOO-eh)	dos (dohs)
3	trois (twah)	tre (tray)	tres (trehs)
4	quatre (kah-truh)	quattro (koo-Aht-troh)	cuatro (kwah-troh)
5	cinq (sank)	cinque (chEEn-ko-eh)	cinco (seen-koh)
6	six (seess)	sei (sEH-ee)	seis (says)
7	sept (seht)	sette (sEHT-teh)	siete (S-Yeh-tay)
8	huit (weet)	otto (OHT-toh)	ocho (OH-choh)
9	neuf (nuhf)	nove (NOH-veh)	nueve (NWEH-bay)
10	dix (deess)	dieci (dee-EH-chee)	diez (dyess)
	Japanese	**German**	**Hawaiian**
1	ichi	ein	e'kahi
2	ni (nee)	zwei	e'lua
3	san	drei	e'kolu

	Japanese	German	Hawaiian
4	shi (she)	vier	e'ha
5	go	funf	e'lima
6	roku	sechs	e'ono
7	shichi	sieben	e'hiku
8	hachi	acht	e'walu
9	ku	neun	e'iwa
10	ju	zehn	'umi

AMAZING MATH TRICKS

The Sum That's Always the Same

Ask someone to give you any number with three digits, but the first digit must be larger than the last. Promise your friend that no matter what number you start with, you can subtract the reverse and then add the reverse of the answer and always come up with the same answer. It works like this:

Step 1: Suppose you start with the number   725
Step 2: Turn that number around   − 527
Step 3: Subtract them   198
Step 4: Turn that number around   + 891
Step 5: Add those numbers   = 1,089

The answer will always be 1,089.

- If the subtraction in step three results in only two digits, put a 0 in front of it like this:

For example: If your number is   221
Reverse and subtract   122
    99
Put a 0 in front   099
Reverse and add   + 990
    1,089

THE GAUSS SHORTCUT

Karl Friedrich Gauss was a world famous mathematician, born in Germany in 1777. When he was only three, he corrected his father's mistakes in arithmetic. At age six, he amazed a teacher who asked him to add up all the numbers from 1 to 100. The answer is 5050, but Gauss came up with the answer so fast that the teacher thought he must have cheated and looked up the answer. But Gauss had only used his own shortcut. He added the numbers from 1 to 100 in pairs that each added up to 101. Then he multiplied the sum by 50.

$1 + 100 = 101$

$2 + 99 \ = 101$

$3 + 98 \ = 101$

and so forth

$48 + 53 = 101$

$49 + 52 = 101$

$50 + 51 = 101 \quad 50 \times 101 = 5050$

Fibonacci Numbers

In 1202, Leonardo Fibonacci discovered this series of numbers that turned out to be a common pattern in nature. The numbers are: 1, 1, 2, 3, 5, 8, 13, 21, 34, 55, 89, 144. Except for the first two numbers, each number is found by adding together the two numbers just before it. For example: $1 + 1 = 2$, $1 + 2 = 3$, $2 + 3 = 5$, $3 + 5 = 8$, $5 + 8 = 13$, $8 + 13 = 21$, $13 + 21 = 34$ etc. If you look at the arrangement of seeds in the head of a sunflower, or on a pine cone, or the arrangement of leaf buds on a stem, you will see the pattern of Fibonacci numbers. When mathematicians follow a formula of Fibonacci numbers, and draw them on a graph, the result is the spiral pattern found in snail shells and animal horns.

Another Lightning-fast Math Trick

Not many people can calculate number problems in their heads. But you can learn some tricks that will amaze people who don't know the secret. Try this one:

Ask someone for a two-digit number that ends in five. Then tell the person that you can multiply that number by itself in your head just as fast as you can write down the answer. Here's the trick:

Step 1: Suppose you start with 35.
Step 2: In your head, you multiply the first digit of your number, which is 3, by the next higher number, which is 4. You'll get 12.
Step 3: Write down the 12, and after it write 25. That's the answer, 1,225.

Ask the person to check your answer on paper or with a calculator. The trick will work with any two-digit number that ends in five.

- Try it again; this time use 85×85.
- Multiply the 8 by the next higher number, which is 9. $8 \times 9 = 72$.
- Write down the 72, after it write 25, and you have the answer, 7,225.

FRACTIONS

It may have been a bookkeeper in Babylonia 5,000 years ago who first used fractions to keep track of grain people gave to the king. He—and it probably would have been a man because in those days women were not taught to read and write—would have

marked his tally in soft clay tablets. Later those tablets were baked until they were hard. In these hard tablets, archeologists have found this symbol, which meant the container was half full:

Apparently the ancient Greeks didn't like to use fractions because they broke up "beautiful numbers." So they let their slaves do all the arithmetic and keep the records. The slaves found fractions to be very useful. The word *fraction* comes from an old Latin word, *fractio*, which means "breaking into pieces."

ROUND NUMBERS

People sometimes "round off" a number. This means, trimming them to the nearest whole ten, hundred, thousand, or million. For example, if you ask how many people went to the soccer game, someone might tell you, "Oh, in round numbers, there must have been a hundred there." If anyone had counted, the accurate number might have been 98 people, or even 120. We round off a lot of numbers. You may learn that the distance around the equator is 25,000 miles. That's a round number. The distance is actually 24,901½ miles, but the rounded number is easier to remember.

DO YOU HAVE TIME TO COUNT TO A MILLION?

If you counted to 100 every minute, and kept counting for eight hours every day, five days a week, it would take you a little over a month to count to 1,000,000.

. . . A BILLION?

If you kept counting at that same rate, it would take you more than eighty *years* to count to 1,000,000,000.

THE ROUNDABOUT NUMBER

142,857 is called the roundabout number because it goes around and around. Look what happens when you multiply 142,857 by 2:

$$142857 \times 2 = 285714$$

All the same digits from the roundabout number are in the answer, but in a different order.

- Try $142857 \times 3 = 428571$. Again, the same digits in different order.
- And $142857 \times 4 = 571428$ . . . same digits, different order!
- Or $142857 \times 5 = 714285$ and $142857 \times 6 = 857142$.
- But if you multiply 142857×7 there's a surprise. It no longer works. You'll get 999999. And it doesn't work with any numbers after 7 either.

MATH SYMBOLS AND SIGNS

+	Add	÷	Divide	<	Less than
−	Subtract	=	Equal	>	Greater than
×	Multiply	≠	Not equal	%	Percent
′	Foot	″	Inch	°	Degree	// Parallel

MATHEMATICIANS WHO CHANGED THE WORLD

Thousands of mathematicians have solved tough problems with ideas so amazing that they truly changed the way we live. Here are three of the most famous.

Archimedes was a great mathematician and scientist who lived in the city of Syracuse, Sicily, about 2,300 years ago. He invented many things, such as a "burning mirror" that worked like a solar furnace to set fire to enemy ships invading the harbor, and a throwing machine called the catapult. The most famous story about him tells of the day he leaped out of his bathtub and ran naked down the street shouting "Eureka!"

One day King Hieron II of Sicily accused a goldsmith of making his crown from a mixture of gold and silver instead of pure gold. The King asked Archimedes to find out if the goldsmith had cheated him—without damaging the crown. Archimedes knew that gold weighs more than silver, and that gold of the same

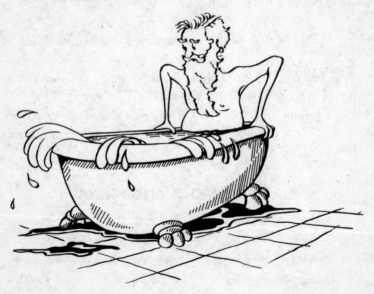

weight as silver has more volume. He knew that a pure gold crown and a piece of pure gold weighing the same would also have the same volume. But what he didn't know was how he could find the volume of a strange-shaped object like the crown. When Archimedes stepped into his bathtub to soak and think about the problem, the water overflowed. Suddenly he realized that his body pushed aside or "displaced" an amount of water equal to his own volume. He could measure the volume of water that spills over the side of the tub and it would be the same volume as the thing in the tub displacing it. That's when he's supposed to have leaped from the tub shouting "Eureka!" (which is the same as "I found it.") and raced to his laboratory.

He dunked the piece of pure gold into a basin of water, and then the crown in a basin of water. The crown caused the water to rise higher, which meant it had greater volume. It was less dense than the gold. It was not pure gold, and the goldsmith was beheaded for cheating the King. From this experience Archimedes went on to discover the principle of bouyancy, which explains why ships float and balloons rise. Using his idea, people from then on could do the new mathematics to find out what would float or sink or fly away.

Sir Isaac Newton was born in Woolsthorpe, Lincolnshire, England, on December 25, 1642. But that was on the old Julian calendar (see page 51). When the world changed to the Gregorian calendar soon after, Newton's birthday was on January 4, 1643. Like Archimedes, Newton was a genius. In fact, he's been called the brightest man who ever lived, even though his teachers didn't think he was so smart because he liked to tinker and make things. He was always hammering away, inventing things in his room. He carved huge sundials on the side of the house, made waterclocks, and a four-wheeled carriage that was powered by the driver.

In those days, people believed that there were two sets of rules: earthly things ran by one set of natural laws, and heavenly things—stars, sun, moon—ran by another. Newton changed all that after he was zonked on the head by an apple one afternoon as he sat under a tree.

No one knows if he really was hit by an apple or not, although that's what Newton told his niece, and she wrote about it in her diary. At any rate, Newton realized that the same force that pulled an apple to the ground was the force that pulled the moon into its orbit around the earth. It was gravity. It seems obvious to us now, of course. But it was an amazing idea then.

From there, Newton went on to work with optics, prisms, light, and color. He built a reflecting telescope. He developed the laws of motion, and the basis of a math called calculus, which is one of science's most important tools.

Albert Einstein must be the most famous school dropout in the world—and certainly the brightest. He was born in Ulm, Germany, on March 14, 1879, and there are dozens of stories about the miserable times Einstein spent in school. He was not stupid at all and, in a way, that was partly to blame for his misery. He didn't like languages or history much, but he loved math and never stopped asking questions. The strict German professors didn't like boys who asked questions, especially questions they had a hard time answering. One teacher told him to leave school because, "You will never amount to anything, Einstein."

But of course, that teacher was dead wrong. In 1921 Albert Einstein won the Nobel Prize for his work in physics. He had developed the Theory of Relativity, which explains the relationships of time and space. His work made it possible to split the atom and create atomic power. During World War II Einstein pleaded with the President of the United States not to drop an atomic bomb on Japan. After the U.S. dropped two bombs,

Einstein worked tirelessly for peace. Space travel is possible because of Albert Einstein's ideas.

If you want to find out more about these three men who changed our world, ask a librarian to help you find books about them. Here are some titles to look for:

Archimedes. Mathematician and Inventor, by Martin Gardner (Macmillan, 1965). An old book but a good one that your library may have.

Isaac Newton. Scientific Genius, by Pearle and Harry Schultz (Garrard, 1972)

Albert Einstein, by Karin Ireland (Silver Burdett Press, 1989)

Einstein, by Nigel Hunter (Watts, 1987)

The Time and Space of Uncle Albert, by Russell Stannard (Henry Holt, 1989). This is not a biography; it is fiction, but it helps you understand what Einstein did. And it's fun to read.

Lucky

CHAPTER TWO

Numbers

Are you lucky? Everyone is sometimes. If you found a dollar on the sidewalk, got 100 on a test, and your mom made your favorite dessert for dinner, you'd say you were lucky that day. But if you lost a dollar, failed the test, and had liver and brussels sprouts for dinner, you'd probably feel unlucky. Luck is something you can't control. It happens by chance.

Who started lucky numbers? No one knows, but it's likely that the earliest people looked at things in nature and saw patterns of numbers. Among Americans today, 43 percent believe that one particular number brings them luck.

ONE

In ancient times, before number systems were invented, people saw there was one sun, one moon, one self, and one became a magical idea. January one is the day for wishing and making resolutions for a good year ahead.

TWO

People also saw the wonderful things that came in pairs: two hands, two eyes, two legs, man and woman, male and female animals, night and day, light and dark, life and death, sickness and health, good and evil. Surely two things must be important, and maybe magic or lucky.

THREE

Three has been a lucky number in almost every age among all kinds of people. "Good things come in threes" is believed as often as "Bad things come in threes."

The ancient Greeks worshiped three principal gods: Zeus, god of the heavens; Poseidon, god of the seas; and Hades, god of the underworld. A Hindu god has three heads. The Christian religion celebrates the Trinity (*tri* means three): Father, Son, and Holy Ghost, and the three graces: faith, hope, and charity.

Other Famous Threes

- Humans are the creatures with body, mind, and spirit.
- All stories have a beginning, a middle, and an end.
- All of life is represented by three: man, woman, and child.
- The life cycle consists of birth, life, and death.
- The world is made up of animal, vegetable, and mineral.
- Three is an important symbol in the Bible, especially the stories of Jonah, who spent three days in the belly of the whale; Daniel, who faced three lions in their den; and Peter, who denied Christ three times.
- People used to believe you could get rid of an evil spell by spinning around three times.
- In the theater, some actors refuse to turn on three lights in the dressing room.

- In gambling casinos, some people walk around the table three times before they begin to play the games.
- We give three cheers, take three chances, get three wishes, and have three strikes before we're out.

Three Wise Monkeys

More than a thousand years ago, Buddhist monks in China taught "See no evil, hear no evil, speak no evil," with drawings of three wise monkeys. One monkey held his paws over his eyes, the second covered his ears, and the third covered his mouth.

Three on a Match

Three cigarettes should never be lit with one match, according to a superstition that began during the Boer War (1899–1902), when the British fought the Afrikaners or Boers in South Africa. Whoever holds the last match is sure to die. The idea made sense at the time. At night, if a British soldier struck a match, a Boer marksman saw it and raised his rifle. He took aim as the second cigarette was lit, and he fired as the match lit the third cigarette.

FOUR

For some people, the symbol of perfection is the square, the foundation of all things. The four corners of the square represent the four elements: earth, water, fire, and air. Life centers around four seasons: spring, summer, fall, and winter. There are four points on the compass: north, south, east, and west. We speak of an honest agreement with someone as a square deal. The four-leaf clover is considered lucky because it represents this honesty. It is also said to represent the four ends of the cross.

FIVE

The ancient Greeks believed that the five-pointed star was magical. We have five senses: sight, hearing, taste, touch, and smell. Our first counting "tool" was the hand with its five fingers. The five-sided shape called the pentagon was believed to have magical qualities. Pythagoras was a great teacher and mathematician in ancient Greece who used the pentagon as the symbol of good luck and good health. Five was the magic number for the Mayan people thousands of years ago. Moslems believe that the outstretched hand with five fingers spread will keep away evil.

SIX

Six is said to be the perfect number because all its factors add up to 6: $1 + 2 + 3 = 6$. It is the symbol of power and protection. The Star of David, made of two inverted triangles, has six points.

SEVEN

Seven has been a lucky number throughout history. Early man saw that the head had seven openings: two eyes, two nostrils, two ears, and one mouth. They knew seven heavenly bodies: the sun, the moon, and five planets, which could be seen without a telescope. They saw seven colors in the rainbow.

Seventh Son of the Seventh Son

The seventh son of a seventh son is said to have the gift of healing, and sometimes "second sight" or the gift of foretelling the future. During the Middle Ages, the seventh son was the one who practiced magic and became a healer.

Only the gypsies believed that the seventh daughter of a seventh daughter also had special powers and that she could foretell the future correctly.

Other Famous Sevens

- Japanese Seven Gods of Luck, who were supposed to sail ships loaded with treasure into harbors on New Year's Eve.
- Seven days of creation, described in the Bible's Book of Genesis; the seventh was a day of rest.
- Seven days in the week.

- Seven deadly sins: pride, covetousness, lust, anger, gluttony, envy, and sloth.
- Seven virtues: faith, hope, charity (love), prudence, justice, fortitude, and temperance.
- Seventh-inning stretch in baseball.
- Seven gifts: wisdom, understanding, counsel, fortitude, knowledge, piety, and fear of the Lord.
- Seventh heaven: An early belief of the Islamic religion says there are seven heavens, one right above the other, getting better as they go higher. The better a person was on earth, the more likely he was to get to the Seventh Heaven. When a person is feeling great, it's a common expression to say, "I'm in Seventh Heaven."
- The Romans believed that every seven years a person's whole body and mind changed completely.
- A broken mirror is supposed to bring seven years' bad luck.
- In Portugal, people used to believe that a woman would have good luck if she wore seven petticoats at one time.
- Seven dwarfs in the Disney version of Snow White: Bashful, Doc, Dopey, Grumpy, Happy, Sleepy, and Sneezy.

The Seven Wonders of the Ancient World

Two hundred years before the birth of Christ, a Greek writer listed the buildings and monuments he thought were the most amazing structures. He chose seven because that was a magic number to the Greek people.

1. The Egyptian Pyramids, which were built more than 4,000 years ago as tombs for the wealthy kings (and leaders). The pyramids are the only one of the ancient wonders still standing.

2. The Colossus of Rhodes, which was an enormous statue of Helios, the sun god, built in the early 200's B.C. after Rhodes had survived a year-long siege. It stood 105 feet high, and straddled the harbor of the city of Rhodes. Ships sailed between its legs. The Colossus was destroyed by an earthquake in 224 B.C.

3. The Hanging Gardens of Babylon, which were great terraces of flowers and trees along the banks of the Euphrates River said to have been built by King Nebuchadnezzar II in the 500's B.C. for one of his wives.

4. The Mausoleum at Halicarnassus, which was the burial place of a king of the Persian empire named Mausolos. Built in the fourth century B.C., the tomb was so large and splendidly decorated that the word *mausoleum* began to be used for all large tombs.

5. The Pharos of Alexandria, which was the world's first lighthouse. Built in the 200's B.C. on the island of Pharos in the harbor of the city of Alexandria in Egypt, it was 400 feet high, with a spiral ramp leading to the top. The light came from a fire fueled with wood.

6. The Statue of Zeus at Olympia, made about 435 B.C. It was 30 feet tall, built of wood, and covered with gold and ivory. Zeus was the highest of Greek gods.

7. The Temple of Artemis at Ephesus, one of the largest temples built by the Greeks. It was built of marble in the sixth century B.C. to honor the goddess of the moon.

Seven Wonders of the Modern World

The editors of the *Reader's Digest Book of Facts* chose the following discoveries and inventions as the seven wonders of today's world:

1. Control of diseases with vaccinations, antibiotics, and other wonder drugs

2. Electric power
3. Space exploration
4. Communications and the processing of information by computers
5. Organ transplants and artificial organs
6. Supermaterials, such as plastics
7. Lasers and other optical technology and microtechnology (such working with electron microscope)

EIGHT

Eight is a symbol of a fresh start. It is seven plus one—good luck and a new beginning.

NINE

The mysterious, magical nine is 3×3.
- A baby grows in its mother for nine months.
- A cat is said to have nine lives.
- There were nine Roman gods.
- People once believed that if you tied nine knots in a piece of black wool, it would cure a sprained ankle.
- A stitch in time saves nine.
- There are said to be nine rivers in the underworld.
- Nine grains of salt were said to get rid of an evil spell.

TEN

Ten was a lucky number to the ancient Romans because the gods had given people ten fingers to count with. Ten is the sum of the first four numbers: $1 + 2 + 3 + 4 = 10$, and therefore had the benefit of all the magic of those numbers.

ELEVEN

Eleven is a lucky number for gamblers, along with seven. When rolling dice, people often say, "Seven, come eleven."

TWELVE

Twelve is not usually thought of as a lucky number, but it is the number of "completeness" for mathematicians because it can be divided by 2, 3, 4, and 6. There are twelve months in a year, twelve signs of the zodiac, two twelves make up the hours of a day.

THIRTEEN

Of all the numbers, thirteen takes first prize for having the most superstitions attached to it. For some people thirteen is lucky; for others, extremely unlucky. There's even a scientific name for the fear of the number thirteen. It's *triskaidekaphobia* (tris-ka-deck-a-foe-be-a).

Most hotels and office buildings have no thirteenth floor. Instead, that floor is called twelve A or fourteen. It's still the thirteenth floor, of course, but at least people aren't reminded of it.

Most Americans may not even realize that thirteen is officially a lucky number. Just look at a one-dollar bill. On the back you'll see a pyramid with thirteen steps. There are thirteen leaves and berries on the olive branch, and the thirteen arrows held by the eagle represent the thirteen original colonies. There are thirteen stars over the eagle's head. It was the Thirteenth Amendment to the Constitution that freed the slaves. The first official flag for the United States had thirteen stripes and thirteen stars, and our first official navy had thirteen ships.

Thirteen at the Table

The big bad belief is about thirteen people at a table. When there are thirteen people seated around a table, one will die before the end of the year, says the superstition. But if everyone joins hands and stands up together, as one, all will be safe. Some say the belief began after the Last Supper, when Judas was the thirteenth guest at the Passover dinner with Jesus and his disciples. Judas was the one who betrayed Jesus.

But there is an even older story in Norse mythology. Twelve Norse gods were invited to dinner, but after everyone was seated, Loki, the god of mischief, arrived. During the dinner, one of the gods was killed.

Lucky Car?

License plate number 13-1313 belonged to William Allen White, a famous newspaperman and writer in Kansas City. When anyone asked why he chose that number, he'd say. "Who'd ever steal a car with such a number?"

Friday the 13th

This is the most feared day of the year. Even people who say they are not superstitious avoid planning weddings or other special events for a Friday the 13th. On the other hand, if you were born on a Friday the 13th, it's a lucky day.

SEVENTEEN

In ancient Greece, the number seventeen was considered unlucky because it came between two "beautiful" numbers, sixteen and eighteen. They liked sixteen because it was equal to 4×4, and four represented the perfect square. Eighteen was okay because it was equal to two nines, and nine was three times the lucky number three.

WHEN YOU SEE A CROW

Some people say:

> *One crow's unlucky*
> *Two's lucky*
> *Three is health*
> *Four is wealth*
> *Five is sickness*
> *And six is death.*

Others say:

> *One crow, sorrow,*
> *Two crows, mirth,*
> *Three crows, a wedding*
> *Four crows, a birth.*

WHAT ARE YOUR CHANCES?

If you buy one ticket to a state lottery, you have one chance in 5,200,000 of being the big winner.

There's one chance in 600,000 that you will be struck by lightning, and your chances of dying from snakebite are one in 3,300,000.

It's too late to worry about it now, but when you were born, you had:

- one chance in 80 of being a twin;
- one chance in 6,400 of being a triplet;
- one chance in 512,000 of being a quadruplet;
- one chance in 40,960,000 for being one of five—a quintuplet.

What Is a 50-50 Chance?

If someone holds out two closed fists and asks you to guess which one holds candy, he might say, "You have a 50-50 chance of being right." He means it is just as likely for the candy to be in one hand as the other. The chances of guessing wrong are also 50-50.

What Is a "Long Shot"?

If you flip ten coins, there's only one chance in a thousand that the coin will land "heads" up ten times in a row. It's a long shot. This saying started in England about 700 years ago when men used bows and arrows. If a town had an archery contest, one target would be put a quarter of a mile away. Hitting that target was a long shot. Not many archers made it. The ones who did were surprised. Since then, we call it a "long shot" when we try something that's not likely to happen.

WHAT'S YOUR LUCKY NUMBER?

Some people use their birthday, or the date that something terrific happened to them, and others just pick a number out of the air. Although some people believe in the "science" of **numerology**, it's not a science at all, but the study of the occult meaning of numbers.

Here is how numerologists figure a person's lucky number. Each letter of the alphabet has a number:

A = 1	H = 8	O = 15	V = 22
B = 2	I = 9	P = 16	W = 23
C = 3	J = 10	Q = 17	X = 24
D = 4	K = 11	R = 18	Y = 25
E = 5	L = 12	S = 19	Z = 26
F = 6	M = 13	T = 20	
G = 7	N = 14	U = 21	

Step 1: Print your name, and under each letter, put the number from the chart, like this:

$$K \quad A \quad T \quad I \quad E \qquad S \quad M \quad I \quad T \quad H \quad E \quad R \quad S$$
$$11 \quad 1 \quad 20 \quad 9 \quad 5 \qquad 19 \quad 13 \quad 9 \quad 20 \quad 8 \quad 5 \quad 18 \quad 19$$

Step 2: Add all the numbers: $11 + 1 + 20 + 9 + 5 + 19 + 13 + 9 + 20 + 8 + 5 + 18 + 19 = 157$

Step 3: Add the numbers of the sum: $1 + 5 + 7 = 13$

Step 4: Add the digits of that sum: $1 + 3 = 4$

Katie Smithers's lucky number is 4. What is yours?

YOUR LUCKY DAY OF THE WEEK

Way back in the sixth century B.C. (about 2,600 years ago) when these numbers were taken seriously, a person found his lucky day from his lucky number. If your lucky number is 1 or 6, there are two lucky days. (Apparently there was a choice. If one day didn't go so well, you could also hope for good luck on other.)

Lucky Number	Lucky Day
1	Saturday or Wednesday
2	Sunday
3	Thursday
4	Monday
5	Tuesday
6	Monday or Friday
7	Thursday
8	Friday
9	Monday

SUPERSTITIONS ABOUT MONEY

- Many people carry a coin made in the year of their birth for good luck. A coin with a hole in the center is also supposed to bring good luck, especially if it's worn around the neck, or on the left side of the body, close to the heart. Many Oriental coins are still made round with a square cut in the center. The circle represents the sky and the square, the earth.
- If you give someone a purse or wallet as a gift, you give good luck with it if you put a shiny new coin or a new dollar bill in it so that the owner will never be without money.
- It is said that if your left hand itches, it is a sign that you're going to receive money.
- When a boat is launched for the first time, sailors often put money under the mast for good luck.
- Some fishermen put a coin in the cork handle of a fishing pole for good luck.

- The groom often gives his bride a penny to wear in her shoe for good luck.
- If someone gives you a scissors or a knife as a gift, you must give that person a coin in exchange if you don't want to cut the friendship.
- Gold was a symbol of the sun, and silver a symbol of the moon. It was the custom in some countries for a woman to wish on the new moon. When she saw the new for the first time, her wish would come true if she bowed to the moon and turned over a silver coin in her pocket.
- The first dollar bill a storeowner receives from a customer is supposed to bring good luck if it is displayed on the wall.

MAKE THE LUCKY PENTAGON . . . AND A SECRET STAR.

A pentagon is a five-sided shape. Members of Pythagoras's secret society believed a pentagon with sides of equal length was a symbol for good luck and good health. Pythagoras even asked his followers to paint the pentagon on the side of their houses after he died so they would remember him.

It's easy to make a pentagon. Cut a strip of paper 1 inch wide from the length of a sheet of typing paper. "Tie" it into an ordinary overhand knot. Pull the ends of the strip just enough to make the knot snug, then flatten the knot. Fold back or cut off the two loose ends. If your paper is thin enough, when you hold up the pentagon to the light you will see a five-pointed star. A pentagon with a five-pointed star inside is called a **pentagram**.

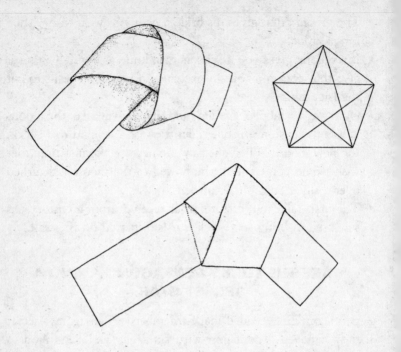

Time

CHAPTER THREE

and Dates

W ho invented the calendar? Why do we have a leap year? Who figured out how to make a clock? What are time zones? Why do we say "o'clock" or A.M. and P.M.? Who named the days of the week? What time is 1300 hours? This chapter brings you up to date on these questions and more.

THE CALENDAR

An easy way to remember the number of days in each month is this old verse:

> Thirty days hath September
> April, June, and November.
> All the rest have thirty-one
> Except February alone,
> Which has twenty-eight days clear
> And twenty-nine in each leap year.

WHAT IS A DAY?

A day is the length of time it takes this planet Earth to spin around once, or twenty-four hours. Scientists say the earth rotates on its axis. The axis is an imaginary pole through the middle of the globe from the North Pole to the South Pole.

More than 3,000 years ago, the Egyptians used star clocks that showed twelve stars or groups of stars as they moved across the sky at night. A person who knew where to look in the night sky could tell the time. The Egyptians also divided the day into twelve parts that were marked by the shadows on a sundial. But the hours didn't become equal and standard until the year 1350, after mechanical clocks had been invented.

WHAT IS A MONTH?

A month is loosely based on the time it takes for the moon to revolve once around the earth. It actually takes 29 days, 12 hours, 44 minutes, and 2.8 seconds.

The months were once called moons. Early humans living in caves saw that twelve new moons appeared between the beginning of one spring and the beginning of the next spring. For thousands of years, people kept track of events by the changes in the moon.

WHAT IS A YEAR?

A year is the length of time it takes the earth to go once around the sun. An official solar year is 365 days, 5 hours, 48 minutes, and 46 seconds, but we call it 365 to make it come out even on the calendar.

Leap Year

Every fourth year one day is added to February to make up for the extra time in the solar year, giving us a year of 366 days. The year "leaps" ahead an extra day. If you happen to be born on February 29 of a leap year, you will have a birthday only once every four years. On the first "anniversary" of your birth date, you'd really be four years old. Most people in that situation celebrate their birthdays every year on February 28 or March 1.

OLD AND NEW CALENDARS

Ancient Babylonian Calendar: This calendar had 354 days in a year, and the year was divided into 12 cycles of the moon. Each moon cycle lasted 29.5 days. But this calendar was 11 days short of the solar year. So the 11 extra days were simply added at the end of each year.

Ancient Egyptian Calendar: This calendar year had 360 days, with 12 months of 30 days each. In this way, they had to add only 5 days at the end of the year.

Ancient Roman Calendar: On the ancient Roman calendar the year started on March 1 because that was the beginning of a farmer's season. It was also when government officials took office. This calendar got hopelessly behind the seasons because it had only 304 days divided into 10 months. Sixty-one days of the solar year were just ignored. Spring, which should have arrived in March, began showing up in the month called May.

Julian Calendar: In the year 46 B.C., the emperor Julius Caesar hired an astronomer, Sosigenes, to make a calendar based on the solar year. The new calendar had 12 months, and each month had 30 or 31 days, except for February, which had 28. The year had 365.25 days. Every fourth year, a day was added, and that year was called leap year.

The Longest Year

The year 46 B.C. had 445 days. It was called "the year of confusion" because Julius Caesar was adding extra days so that when his new Julian calendar began, it would match the seasons. In 45 B.C., spring started at the right time.

Gregorian Calendar: In 1582, Pope Gregory XIII changed the Julian calendar. The seasons had gotten off again because the Julian calendar was actually 11 days and 14 seconds longer than the solar year. He kept a Leap Year every four years, but he declared that the year beginning a new century should not be a leap year unless it could be divided by 400. This is the calendar we still use today. It is off by only 16 seconds a year, and only falls out of step with the seasons a bit every 3,323 years.

World Calendar: Some people want everyone in the world to use a newer, more sensible calendar divided into four equal parts of 13 weeks each. A "world day" would be added at the end of December for a total of 365 days. In leap years another world day would be added at the end of June. With this system, we would use the same calendar every year. If you were born on a Tuesday, for example, your birthday would always be on that Tuesday. Halloween would still be on October 31, but it would always fall on the same day of the week.

The Mystery of the Missing 11 Days

If you look in American or English history books, you may find that nothing happened between September 3 and September 13 in 1752. Why not? Was everyone asleep? Well, sort of. It was in 1752 that England and her American colonies began to use the Gregorian calendar, and on their old Julian calendar they were eleven days behind. In order to catch up, they skipped from September 2 to September 14.

Benjamin Franklin wrote how nice it was ". . . for those who love their pillow to lie down in Peace on the second of this month and not perhaps awake until the morning of the fourteenth."

NAMES OF THE MONTHS

The names of the months come from the ancient Roman calendar. The last four months got their names from the Latin numbers 7 to 10 because the ancient Romans started their year in spring with the month of March.

Modern Calendar	Roman Calendar
January	Janurius (Janus, god of gateways)
February	Februarius (Febra, festival of purification)
March	Martius (Mars, god of war)
April	Aprilis (*aperio*, Latin for "to open" as in buds opening)
May	Maius (Maia, goddess of fertility)
June	Junius (Juno, goddess of women)
July	Julius (Julius Caesar)
August	Augustus (Augustus Caesar)
September	September (*septem*, seven)
October	October (*octo*, eight)
November	November (*novem*, nine)
December	December (*decem*, ten)

Quintilis was the name of the fifth month, as long as the year started in March. In 44 B.C., Quintilis was changed to Julius (July) to honor the emperor, Julius Caesar.

In the year 8 B.C., Sextilis, the sixth month, was changed to Augustus (August) to honor Augustus Caesar, the first Roman emperor. But July had 31 days, and August had only 30. That wouldn't do! The emperors had to have equal numbers. So a day was borrowed from February, and both July and August have since had 31 days.

DAYS OF THE WEEK

The days of the week we use now came from the language of ancient Saxons in England. The days were named for the planets and gods.

Our Days	Saxon Days
Sunday	Sun's day
Monday	Moon's day
Tuesday	Tiw's day
Wednesday	Woden's day
Thursday	Thor's day
Friday	Frigg's day
Saturday	Saterne's day

COUNTING THE SECONDS IN A YEAR

Our calendar is 26 seconds off each year. Not much time, but it adds up.

- 1 second is 0.0000116 parts of a day.
- There are 86,400 seconds in a day.
- There are 604,800 seconds in a week.
- There are 31,536,000 seconds in a year.
- And 31,622,400 seconds in a leap year.

- Each day is 0.00000002 seconds longer than the one before because the earth is gradually slowing down.

WHY 60 MINUTES, 60 SECONDS?

Five thousand years ago, the Sumerian people used a number system based on 60. From that same number system, astronomers divided each hour of the day into 60 parts. The long lines of longitude on the globe (see page 89) are measured in degrees of 60.

Later, Latin astronomers called these parts *pars minuta*, which meant "the little part of an hour." That term was shortened to minute. The second division was the separation of minutes into 60 parts, or *pars secunda*, which became seconds.

THE OFFICIAL TICK

The official second keeps ticking on an atomic clock (see page 64). If you would like to hear the atomic second tick away, call WWV, the National Bureau of Standard's radio station. The number is (303) 499-7111. WWV will also give you the time in Greenwich, England, using the 24 hour, military time system (see page 58).

Time on the atomic clock is divided into **nanoseconds**. Each nanosecond is equal to .0000000001 second.

WHAT DO THESE TIME TERMS MEAN?

A.M: These initials stand for the Latin phrase *ante meridiem*, or before noon. When you say, "I'll be there at 8 A.M.," you mean you will be there at eight o'clock in the morning. When you say 12 A.M., you mean midnight.

P.M.: These initials mean *post meridiem*, or after noon. "I'll meet you at 2 P.M." means "I'll meet you at two o'clock in the afternoon."

A.D.: These initials stand for the Latin phrase *anno domini*, which means the year of our Lord. It refers to the time after the birth of Christ. The year 1186 A.D. means it was 1,186 years after the birth of Christ.

B.C.: This means before the time of Christ. A date such as 400 B.C. was not 400 years ago. It means 400 years before the birth of Christ, and you have to add it to the present year if you want to find out how long ago that was. *For example:* 400 + 1992 = 2,392 years ago.

B.C. 400 300 200 100 0 100 200 300 400 A.D.

Fortnight: This is an old-fashioned way of saying two weeks or fourteen days.

O'clock: This is a short way of saying "of the clock." We say ten o'clock instead of saying "the time is ten of the clock."

Time Immemorial: This means a time before anyone can remember. Long ago, someone decided that the year 1189 A.D. was "the time beyond which the memory of man runs not to the contrary."

Once in a Blue Moon: People sometimes say that a thing happens once in a blue moon when they mean it hardly ever happens. Every month we see a full moon, but once a year a second full moon appears in the same month. The saying refers to the rare time when that second full moon looks blue because of dust in the atmosphere. One famous blue moon, seen on

September 26, 1950, was caused by clouds of dust from Canadian forest fires.

WHAT IS A SOLSTICE?

It is the name given to the day on which the sun is farthest from the equator as the earth rotates around the sun. There are two each year. The **summer solstice** is on June 21, which is the longest day of the year and the shortest night. The **winter solstice** occurs on December 22, the shortest day and the longest night. Those days mark the beginning of summer and winter.

WHAT IS AN EQUINOX?

Twice a year, when the sun crosses the equator, the day and night are of equal length. The **spring equinox**, the first day of spring, is on March 21. The **autumnal equinox**, the first day of autumn, is September 23.

WHY IS EASTER ON A DIFFERENT DATE EACH YEAR?

Figuring out your Easter school vacation or spring break can be confusing. In the year 325 A.D., Easter was officially declared as the first Sunday after the first full moon after the spring equinox on March 21. Since the cycles of the moon are not in sync with the solar calendar, Easter can occur on any Sunday between March 22 and April 25.

WHAT IS GROUNDHOG DAY?

Groundhog Day is February 2. Tradition has it that if the ground-hog comes out of its hole and sees its shadow on February 2, spring will be another six weeks away. But if it's cloudy, and he sees no

shadow, spring will come sooner. (Actually, groundhogs hibernate in a deep sleep. When, or if, they stagger out to look around on February 2, it's not to look for shadows, but to look for a mate or get something to eat.) This tradition came to America with people from England and Germany. In England, February 2 is a Christian celebration called Candlemas, the day when Jesus was presented in the Temple. If the weather is sunny on Candlemas, it is said that winter will remain a while. If it is cloudy, spring will come soon. In Germany, badgers were said to predict the weather at this time. German settlers in Pennsylvania had no badgers, but they had groundhogs, also called woodchucks.

One expert figured out that the groundhog named Puxatawny Phil has predicted spring's arrival correctly only 28 percent of the time.

MILITARY TIME

When an officer in a war movie tells his men to be ready at 1700 hours, what time does he mean? To be on time, those soldiers will have to be ready at five o'clock in the afternoon. Military time uses a 24-hour clock. It doesn't repeat numbers or use A.M. or P.M. The day begins at 0000, which is 12:00 A.M. or midnight on civilian clocks. It ends at 2400 hours, or midnight again. Noon is 1200 hours; 1 P.M. is 1300 hours, 2 P.M. is 1400 hours, and so on. Instead of eight o'clock, a military person says, "Oh-800." For three o'clock, he says "fifteen hundred hours." The advantage of military time is that there is no confusion. In the tension of battle, there is no chance of mixing up A.M. and P.M.

What time do you get up in the morning, by military time?

What time does your school day end, by military time?

Ship's Bells

On ships, the 24-hour day is divided into six "watches." Each watch lasts 4 hours. One watch starts at 0000 to 0004 (midnight to 4 A.M.); second watch is 0004 to 0008; and so on around the clock. Signals are given by the ship's bell, which sounds every half hour. One bell rings after the first half hour; two bells for the second half hour. When the bell rings eight times, that signals the end of one four-hour watch, and the bell signals start over.

TIME ZONES

You decide to call your grandmother in San Diego at 8:00 one Saturday morning from your house in Cleveland. The phone rings and rings, and finally she answers. She sounds like she's half asleep when she says, "Do you know it's five o'clock in the morning?"

You have to remember time zones. Originally, cities in this country established their own time in reference to the sun. When the sun was straight overhead, it was noon. But the railroad companies hated that system because every stop along the route had a different time. Finally the big railroad companies in the United States insisted on having a "standard time." They persuaded the U.S. Naval Observatory and Western Union Telegraph Company to begin sending the "correct" time by telegraph, and at noon on Sunday, November 18, 1883, the whole country went onto the same clock. The first International Meridian Conference in 1884 made it official. From that time on, the trains appeared according to a standard time schedule.

Standard time was possible because the conference set up world-wide time zones to create regular time changes. Lines were

Standard Time Zones in Continental United States

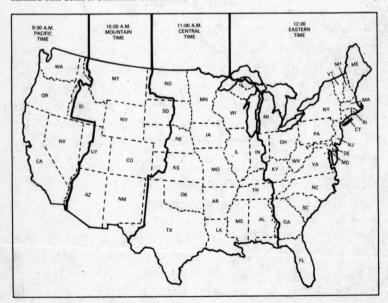

drawn every 15 degrees longitude on the map of the earth. The 15 degrees is the distance the earth rotates in one hour. Each time zone is one hour earlier than the one to the east of it. The zones begin at the prime meridian or 0 degrees of longitude, which runs through Greenwich, England. There are twenty-four international time zones. North America is divided into eight international time zones: Newfoundland, Atlantic, Eastern, Central, Mountain, Pacific, Yukon, and Alaskan. Sometimes a time zone line has to zigzag a little to go around small towns or countries to avoid dividing them into two time zones.

Breakfast When?

When people in Los Angeles are eating breakfast at 9 A.M. on a Sunday . . .

New Yorkers are eating lunch at 12 noon . . .

and people in Paris, France, are having Sunday dinner at 6 P.M. . . . and in Bangkok, someone is having a midnight snack at 12 A.M. . . . and in Tokyo, most people are asleep because it is 2:00 on Monday morning!

International Date Line

The International Date Line is an imaginary line set at 180 degrees longitude, right in the middle of the Pacific Ocean. It marks the place where time makes a 24-hour jump, instead of just 1 hour. If you travel around the world from east to west, you lose a day. When you come back, west to east, you get that day back. If you set out from California to Japan on Monday, it will be Tuesday when you cross the Date Line. Going the other way, Tuesday becomes Monday.

Odd Zones

The Commonwealth of Independent States, which, for the most part, used to be the U.S.S.R., is so big that it covers eleven time zones.

China is just as big. It also extends over eleven time zones, but China only uses one. The government wants all its people on the same time, even if the morning sun may appear at 6 A.M. on the coast and eleven hours later over on the far side of the country.

Israel, for religious reasons, keeps to a time schedule two hours behind other countries in that same time zone.

DAYLIGHT SAVING TIME

On the first Sunday of April, we turn our clocks ahead one hour for Daylight Saving Time. On the last Sunday of October, we turn them back an hour. This system began in 1916, during World War I, as a way of saving energy. The government reasoned that farmers could work longer hours in the field if it stayed light longer in the evening, and people in factories wouldn't need to turn lights on as early.

Hawaii and parts of Indiana do not use Daylight Saving Time. In Arizona, only the Navajo Reservation uses DST.

It's easy to remember how to change the clock if you keep in mind, "Spring ahead; Fall back." In spring, you move the clock ahead an hour, making it one hour later; in fall, you move it back again, making it an hour earlier.

SPACE YEARS

- Mercury has four years packed into our one because that planet zips around the sun four times in one Earth year.

- If you could live on Mars, you'd have to wait 687 days for your birthday to come around because that's how long a year is on that planet.
- One year on Jupiter is equal to 247 years on Earth.
- Neptune's year is equal to 164.8 years on Earth.
- And it would take 247 Earth years to make one year on Pluto.

GEOLOGIC TIME

Geologic time records the history of Earth. This planet is more than 4 billion years old. Scientists have found the fossil remains of life from a quarter of a billion years ago, which is only the last quarter of earth's history. Human beings have been around only the last 2 million years.

Geologic time is measured in eras, epochs, and ages. An **era** is a huge chunk of time. Millions of years of earth's history are marked by the different kinds of plants and animals that lived then. A **period** is a smaller section of time that marks the changes in the environment. **Ages** are still smaller sections of time named for the creatures that dominated the earth then, such as the Age of Reptiles; or a time of big changes on the earth, such as the Ice Age; or a time marked by the kinds of tools made by humans, such as the Stone Age or the Iron Age.

KEEPING TIME

Hour Glass: This was an early way of keeping track of time as grains of sand dropped through the narrow neck of a glass funnel into another chamber below. At the end of an hour, all the sand would have dropped into the bottom chamber and the glass would be turned over. A small version of an hour glass called an egg timer keeps track of a minute. To make a three-minute egg, you'd have to turn the egg timer over twice.

Water Clock: A water clock is a bucket with the evenly spaced marks down the inside to tell the hour. Water drips out of a small hole in the bottom of the bucket. You tell the time by looking at the level of water in the bucket.

Sundial: A sundial is a circle of twelve evenly spaced marks, and a raised wedge in the center. As the sun moves across the sky, the shadow of the wedge falls on the time markers. The sundial was the first continuous time piece, but it wasn't very helpful on cloudy days.

A Candle Clock was simply a candle with hours marked on its side. It took an hour for the candle to burn down from one mark to the next.

Pendulum Clocks were the most accurate way of measuring time up to the 1900s. A pendulum one meter long takes one second to swing in a full arc from one side to the other. The swing of a shorter pendulum is controlled by gears. A Dutch clockmaker, Christiaan Huygens, made the first pendulum clock in 1654.

Quartz Clocks are common today. Such a clock is based on the vibrations of a quartz crystal. The speed of the vibrations is controlled by an electrical circuit from a battery.

Atomic Clock. This is the most accurate clock ever made. It is based on tiny vibrations of an atom that vibrates 9,192,631,770 times each second—without fail.

YEAR OF THE DRAGON

The Chinese people name the years, as well as days and months. Each year is named for an animal: Rat, Ox, Tiger, Hare, Dragon, Snake, Horse, Sheep, Monkey, Rooster, Dog, and Pig. When

the cycle of animals is finished, it starts all over again. The year 2000 will be the Year of the Dragon.

RAT	OX	TIGER	HARE	DRAGON	SNAKE
1984	1985	1986	1987	1988	1989
1996	1997	1998	1999	2000	2001

HORSE	SHEEP	MONKEY	ROOSTER	DOG	PIG
1990	1991	1992	1993	1994	1995
2002	2003	2004	2005	2006	2007

MAJOR HOLIDAYS IN THE UNITED STATES

January	1 New Year's Day
	15 Martin Luther King, Jr.'s birthday
	19 Robert E. Lee's birthday, celebrated in southern states
	20 Inauguration Day, every four years
February	2 Groundhog Day
	12 Abraham Lincoln's birthday
	14 Valentine's Day
	22 George Washington's birthday
March	17 St. Patrick's Day

March or April		Easter Sunday
April	1	April Fool's Day
May	1	May Day
2nd Sunday		Mother's Day
	30	Memorial Day
June	14	Flag Day
3rd Sunday		Father's Day
July	4	Independence Day
September		
1st Monday		Labor Day
October	12	Columbus Day
	31	Halloween
November		
1st Tues. after		
1st Monday		Election Day
	11	Veterans Day
4th Thursday		Thanksgiving Day
December	25	Christmas Day

MAJOR HOLIDAYS IN CANADA

January 1	New Year's Day
March or April	Good Friday
1st Mon. before May 25	Victoria Day
July 1	Canada Day
1st Mon. in September	Labor Day
2nd Mon. in October	Thanksgiving Day
November 11	Remembrance Day
December 25	Christmas Day
December 26	Boxing Day

Boxing Day began in England. On the first weekday after Christmas, people "boxed" gifts for employees, postmen, and others who served the community.

HOW LONG WILL YOU BE IN SCHOOL?

From kindergarten until you graduate from high school, kids in most states will be in school 2,405 days or . . .

16,835 hours or . . .

1,010,100 minutes or . . .

60,606,000 seconds.

WHICH WOULD BE BETTER . . .

. . . a broken watch, or a watch that ran ten seconds slow every day? The broken watch is actually better because it would show the right time at least twice each day. But the watch that runs slow would tell the right time only once in 11.8 years.

Weights

CHAPTER FOUR

and Measures

After people learned to count, they began to use numbers to weigh and measure things. At first they used odd measurements—a hank, a heer, a stade, and a butt, for example. But the weights and measures we use today would probably surprise our ancient ancestors. Would they know what we mean when we measure with a decibel, a hertz, a nanometer, or a parsec?

THE FIRST SCALE

The first scale for weighing things was only a stick hanging from a rope, with two smaller ropes hanging from each end. The things to be weighed were tied to the ropes. When the items were of equal weight, the stick balanced parallel to the ground. This system was used 7,000 years ago by the Egyptians. Then about 5,000 years ago, someone in Egypt had a good idea. Why not have some weights of known amounts to hang on one end of the scale? And that worked fine. Some of those first weights were stones, seeds, or grain.

THE EARLIEST KNOWN WEIGHTS

Mina: This weight of about 21 ounces was used in Babylon. Minas were made in different shapes to denote different amounts. A 5 mina weight was shaped like a duck. A 30 mina weight was shaped like a swan. If someone wanted to weigh out 30 minas of grain, he put a swan weight on one side of the scale, and poured grain into the other side of the scale. When the grain balanced with the mina swan, the buyer knew he was getting 5 minas.

Talent: This Greek measurement equaled about 56.9 pounds.

Carat: The first carat was a small bean or *karob* that weighed 4 grains of wheat. We still use the carat today. Now it equals 3.086 grains, and is used to weigh precious stones and metals. When you see gold marked 14 carat, you know the gold is 14 parts gold and 10 parts of some other metal. Pure gold (24 carat) is so soft that other metals are added to make it more durable.

Goose Quills and Gold Dust: Gold dust was so light that Egyptians used to measure it by the amount that would fit into a goose quill.

THE FIRST MEASUREMENTS OF LENGTH

The first measurements were based on parts of the human body. They were easy to use and always handy, but they varied from one person to another because no two people are exactly the same size. Even so, these measurements lasted for centuries, and we still use some of them today.

Digit: The width of a finger, or about ¾ inch.

Hand: The width of a grown man's hand, about four inches. The height of a horse is still measured in hands.

Span: From the end of a grown man's thumb to his little finger when his fingers are spread out. A span is about 9 inches.

Inch: For many years an inch was the width of an adult man's thumb. In the 1300s, King Edward II of England declared that an inch was equal to three grains of barley laid end to end.

Foot: The length of an adult man's foot, about 12 inches. The Greeks and Romans must have had smaller feet than men today because their "foot" only measured 11½ inches instead of 12.

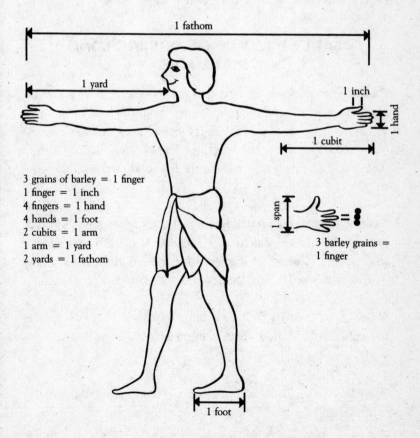

3 grains of barley = 1 finger
1 finger = 1 inch
4 fingers = 1 hand
4 hands = 1 foot
2 cubits = 1 arm
1 arm = 1 yard
2 yards = 1 fathom

3 barley grains = 1 finger

Yard: The length of the belt of an Anglo-Saxon (English) man was once a yard. In the 1100s, King Henry I of England declared that the yard would be the measurement from the tip of his nose to the end of his thumb when his arm was stretched out.

Cubit: A cubit was the distance from a man's elbow to his fingertips, about 21 inches. Noah's Ark was measured in cubits: 300 cubits long, 50 cubits wide, and 30 cubits high. By today's measurements, the Ark would have been 525 feet, as long as one football field plus three-quarters of another one. It would have been almost 88 feet wide and 53 feet high.

EARLY WAYS OF MEASURING LONG DISTANCES

Pace: The pace was an Egyptian measurement. It was the distance covered in a full step, measured from the heel of one foot to the toe of that same foot as it stepped back down—about 5 feet. Today, a pace is the length of a single step, about 2½ to 3 feet. You can "pace off" a distance if you know how long your step is.

Stade: Also an Egyptian measurement, a stade was equal to 100 paces. The Greeks called it a *stadion*. The Romans called it *stadian*, and it was also the word for the length of a foot race. The English word *stadium* comes from stade, stadion, and stadian.

Mile: A mile was 1,000 paces of a Roman soldier, which was the equivalent of 5,280 feet, a measurement we still use.

ODD AND OLD MEASURING TERMS

Ell: A measurement for cloth. The cloth was measured from a person's hand, around the elbow, and back to the hand. King Edgar of England standardized the ell at 36 inches, which is a yard.

Butt: A large cask used for shipping wine. It held 130 gallons. The word *butt* became the basis for the word *bottle*.

Rod: The length of the left feet of the first sixteen men to come out of church, as they lined up heel to toe. In the 1500s, Queen Elizabeth I declared the rod to be 16½ feet.

Ro: A measurement for liquids. In ancient Egypt, the ro was equal to 1 mouthful. In the English system, 2 ro = 1 jigger; 2 jiggers = 1 jack; 2 jacks = 1 jill; 2 jills = 1 cup; 2 cups = 1 pint; 2 pints = 1 quart; 2 quarts = 1 pottle; 2 pottles = 1 gallon; 2 gallons = 1 pail; 2 pails = 1 peck; 2 pecks = 1 bushel; 2 bushels = 1 strike; 2 strikes = 1 coomb; 2 coombs = 1 cask; 2 casks = 1 barrel; 2 barrels = 1 hogshead; 2 hogsheads = 1 pipe; 2 pipes = 1 tun.

In the 1600s, when the measurement called the jack was discontinued, the nursery rhyme "Jack and Jill" was written. In it, the writer is saying that if the jack isn't going to be used anymore, the jill will be the next measure to be thrown out.

> *Jack and Jill went up the hill*
> *To fetch a pail of water.*
> *Jack fell down and broke his crown*
> *And Jill came tumbling after.*

THE ENGLISH SYSTEM

In the United States today we use what is known as the English system of measurement, which is based on a mixture of Greek, Roman, and Babylonian systems.

Length

1 inch = 0.083 feet
1 foot = 12 inches
1 yard = 3 feet
1 rod = 5.5 yards
1 furlong = 40 rods
1 mile (on land) = 8 furlongs, or 5,280 feet

Area

1 square inch = 0.007 square feet
1 square foot = 144 square inches
1 square yard = 9 square feet
1 square rod = 30¼ square yards
1 acre = 160 square rods
1 square mile = 640 acres
1 township = 36 square miles

Liquid Measure (capacity)

1 gill = ¼ pint
1 pint = 4 gills
1 quart = 2 pints
1 gallon = 4 quarts
1 barrel = 31.5 gallons

Cooking Measure

1 teaspoon = ⅛ fluid ounce
1 tablespoon = 3 teaspoons, or ½ fluid ounce
1 fluid ounce = 2 tablespoons, or 6 teaspoons
1 cup = 16 tablespoons, or 8 fluid ounces
1 pint = 2 cups, or 16 fluid ounces
1 quart = 2 pints, or 32 ounces
1 gallon = 4 quarts, or 16 cups

Dry Measure (capacity)

1 pint = ½ quart
1 quart = 2 pints
1 peck = 8 quarts
1 bushel = 4 pecks

THREE SEPARATE ENGLISH SYSTEMS
FOR MEASURING WEIGHT

Avoirdupois Weight

Avoirdupois (a-ver-de-poiz) is a French word that means "goods of weight." We use avoirdupois weight to weigh everything but medicines and precious metals and stones.

A *grain* is the smallest unit of avoirdupois weight. It was based on the weight of a single grain of wheat. *Dram* is an ancient Greek word that meant handful.

1 grain = 0.002285 ounces
1 dram = $27^{11}/_{32}$ grains
1 ounce = 16 drams, or 437.5 grains
1 pound = 7,000 grains, or 16 ounces
1 hundredweight = 100 pounds
1 ton = 2,000 pounds, or 20 hundredweights
1 long hundredweight = 112 pounds
1 long ton (or gross) = 20 long hundredweights, or 2,240 pounds

Troy Weight

This system is used to measure precious metals and stones. The word *troy* is said to come from Troyes, France, where this system of measurement originated. The smallest troy unit is also the *grain*, which weighs the same as the avoirdupois grain.

1 grain = 0.002083 troy ounces
1 carat = 3.086 grains
1 pennyweight = 24 grains (the weight of the original English penny)
1 troy ounce = 20 pennyweights, or 480 grains
1 troy pound = 12 troy ounces, or 5,760 grains

Apothecaries' Measure

This system is used to measure medicines. Apothecary is the old-fashioned name for a pharmacy or drugstore. Apothecaries' weights are based on troy weights, and the pound, ounce, and grain are the same.

Apothecaries also have some separate fluid measures in addition to the standard ones.

Weight:
1 scruple = 20 grains
1 dram = 3 scruples
1 apothecaries' ounce = 8 drams, or 480 apothecaries' grains
1 apothecaries' pound = 12 apothecaries' ounces, or 5,760 grains
Fluid Measure:
1 minim (or drop) = ⅟₆₀ fluid dram, or ⅛ fluid ounce
1 fluid dram = 60 minims
1 fluid ounce = 8 fluid drams

WHICH WEIGHS MORE, A POUND OF FEATHERS OR A POUND OF GOLD?

Everyone thinks this is a trick question and that the answer is, "They weigh the same . . . a pound is a pound, no matter what you're weighing." But what you're weighing makes a difference, and the two "pounds" are not the same, at least not in the United States. Gold is measured in troy weight. A pound of gold by troy weight is equal to 5,760 grains. A pound of feathers is measured by avoirdupois weight, and is equal to 7,000 grains. So a pound of feathers weighs more than a pound of gold.

WHY DO WE USE LB. TO MEAN POUND?

It comes from the Roman word *libra*, which was a unit of weight equivalent to 1/125th of an Egyptian talent. Later, when the English called that weight a pound, they kept the *l* and *b* (lb.) from libra.

GETTING WEIGHED

When you stand on a scale to find out how much you weigh, you are actually finding out how great the pull of earth's gravity is on your body. The pull of gravity on the surface of the earth is termed 1 G. 2 G is twice the pull of gravity. If you weigh 100 pounds at 1 G, you will weigh 200 pounds at 2 G. When astronauts ride the rockets into space, they feel heavier and heavier as these G forces push them back against their seats. At 4 or 5 Gs, humans feel uncomfortable. But astronauts can stand the pressure up to 10 Gs long enough for their space ship to ride the rocket as it breaks away from earth's force of gravity. To do that, the rocket has to travel at least 25,000 miles per hour.

Because the moon is smaller than the earth, it has a smaller gravitational pull. If an astronaut weighs 180 pounds on the earth, he will weigh only 28 pounds on the moon.

On July 16, 1969, astronauts Buzz Aldrin and Neil Armstrong were the first humans to walk on the moon. But they didn't really

walk—they leaped and hopped and jumped 5 or 6 feet off the moon's surface with every step because they were pulled down by less gravity than on earth.

LAND UNITS

Acre: An acre is 4,840 square feet. Originally it was the amount of land a yoke of oxen could plow in a day. King Henry VIII set an acre at 40 rods by 40 rods.

Furlong: A furlong was the length of a plowed field, about 660 feet or 40 rods. Six furlongs = 1 mile.

Homestead: 160 acres. When the pioneers went west, they were given 160 acres to settle as homesteads.

Township: 36 square miles. Maps used to be marked off in townships.

What's an Acre in Japan?

If you buy a tan in Japan or a bunder in the Netherlands, it's not the same as an acre in the United States.

Japan: tan = 0.2449 acres
Spain: aranzada = 1.038 acres
Egypt: fedden = 1.038 acres
Italy: quadrato = 1.25 acres
Netherlands: bunder = 100 acres
Philippines: balita = 0.69 acres

THE METRIC SYSTEM

The metric system was invented by French mathematicians in 1790 as a simpler, more commonsensical way of measuring than using body parts and other irregular amounts. In the metric system all units of measure are based on the number 10. The United States is one of the few nations of the world that doesn't use the metric system. Scientists around the world all use metric measurements so that their measurements will be standard.

The Meter

French scientists measured the distance from the North Pole to the equator and decided to use one ten-millionth (1/10,000,000) of that distance as the new standard length, which they called the meter. The meter is the basis for all the metric measures of volume, weight, surface area, and so on. Unfortunately, the instruments used in the 1700s to measure that distance from the pole to the equator were not very accurate. The calculations were a little off. But the meter was well established by the time the mistake was discovered, so it wasn't changed. One meter is equal to 39.37 inches.

The official meter stick is made of platinum. It is kept at the International Bureau of Weights and Measures in Paris. The United States keeps its official meter stick at the National Bureau of Standards in Gaithersburg, Maryland. It has twice been compared with the meter stick in Paris and found to be a little off. But any metal contracts and expands a tiny amount, even when it is kept where temperature and humidity are carefully controlled. In 1889, our meter stick was 1.49 micrometers off, and in 1957 it was 1.45 micrometers off. A micrometer is one-millionth of a meter, so the meter stick wasn't off by much. But it was enough to make many meter sticks inaccurate.

In 1960, scientists declared the official measure of a meter to be 1,650,763.73 wavelengths of krypton light. Krypton is a gas used in high-powered, tungsten-filament light bulbs, like neon gas is used in neon lights. A wavelength is a better measurement than platinum because it is easy to make, and it is accurate up to one hundred-millionth (1/100,000,000) of an inch.

The Liter

The liter measures volume, or size. A liter is equal to a cube with each side one-tenth of a meter long. One-tenth of a liter is called a deciliter. One liter contains 1 cubic decimeter of water, and equals 1.057 quarts. In Canada and other countries using the metric system, milk, gas, and other liquids are sold by the liter instead of by the quart or gallon.

The Kilogram

The weight of water that would fill 1 cubic decimeter is the unit called a kilogram. One kilogram is equal to 2.2046 pounds.

The Magic Number Ten

The metric system is based on multiples and subdivisions of the number ten. The names of the units of measure are formed by adding "*prefixes*" to the name of the basic unit. (A *prefix* is a word attached to the front of another word as a way of adding to the meaning of the word.) For example, the prefix *deka-* means ten times. A dekameter is ten times 1 meter, or 10 meters. *Deci-* means one-tenth of. A deciliter is one-tenth of a liter.

Prefix	Meaning	Example
Mega-	1 million times	megameter, megaliter, megagram
Kilo-	1,000 times	kilometer, kilogram
Hecto-	100 times	hectometer
Deka-	10 times	dekaliter
Deci-	$\frac{1}{10}$ of	decimeter
Centi-	$\frac{1}{100}$ of	centimeter
Milli-	$\frac{1}{1,000}$ of	milligram
Micro-	$\frac{1}{1,000,000}$ of	micrometer

Other Prefixes

Exa = 1,000,000,000,000,000,000 times (written as 10^{18}, which means ten to the 18th power)

Peta = 10 to the 15th power, or 15 zeros

Tera = 10 to the 12th power, or 12 zeros

Giga = 10 to the 9th power, or 9 zeros

Myria = 10,000 times

Mega = 1 million times

Nano = 1 billionth of

Pic = 1 trillionth of

Femto = 10 to the minus 15th power, or 15 zeros

Atto = 10 to the minus 18th power, or 18 zeros

Metric Measures Compared to English Measures

1 hectare = 2.47 acres

1 kilometer = 0.62 miles

1 meter = 39.37 inches

1 centimeter = 0.39 inches

1 millimeter = 0.04 inches

1 kilogram = 2.2046 pounds

1 gram = 0.035 ounce

1 milligram = 0.02 grain
1 liter = 1.057 quarts
1 milliliter = .034 fluid ounces

Changing Metric Measures to English Measures

To change an English measurement into the metric system, multiply it by the number in the following chart.

For example: If you know your desk is 42 inches long, and you want to find out how many centimeters long it is, multiply 42 inches by 2.54.

42 × 2.54 = 106.68 centimeters

English measurement	× this number =	metric measurement
acres	0.40	hectares
miles	1.6	kilometers
yards	0.9	meters
feet	0.3	meters
feet	30	centimeters
inches	2.54	centimeters
gallons	3.8	liters
quarts	0.95	liters
cups	0.24	liters
ounces (fluid)	30	milliliters
ounces (dry)	28.3	grams
tons	0.9	metric tons
pounds	0.45	kilograms
tablespoons	15	milliliters
teaspoons	5	milliliters

SPACED-OUT MEASUREMENTS: ASTRONOMICAL MEASUREMENTS

Astronomical Unit: The distance from Earth to Sun is 92,900,000 miles. That distance is called the Astronomical Unit, or AU. The Astronomical Unit is used to measure distances in our solar system.

Mercury = 0.4 AU from the sun
Venus = 0.7 AU
Earth = 1 AU
Mars = 1.5 AU
Jupiter = 5.2 AU
Saturn = 9.6 AU
Uranus = 19.2 AU
Neptune = 30.1 AU
Pluto = 39.4 AU

Light Year: A light year is the distance light travels in one year in a vacuum. Space is a vacuum—it has no air, no atmosphere. Light years are used to measure distances in our galaxy. One light year = 5,878,000,000,000 miles (nearly 6 trillion miles). Light travels at a speed of 186,300 miles per second.

Parsec: Astronomers also measure distance with the parsec, which is equal to 3.259 light years.

Old Light

The closest stars are 25 trillion miles away. Light from those stars has been traveling 4½ years before we see it.

The farthest thing in space that we can see without a telescope is the Spiral Nebula in the constellation Andromeda. It is

2,200,000 light years away. That means the light we see from Andromeda now, left that constellation 2,200,000 years ago. If one night we could no longer see Andromeda, it would mean that the light had stopped—the stars died—2,200,000 years ago.

HOW MANY STARS IN THE SKY?

Astronomers say there are at least 10 billion galaxies. If each galaxy is anything like the Milky Way galaxy that we are part of, then there must be about 10 sextillion or 10,000,000,000,000,000,000,000 stars in the universe.

HOW MANY GRAINS OF SAND IN ALL THE BEACHES ON EARTH?

There are far more grains of sand than stars in the sky. Physicist Charles James figured it this way: If 100,000 grains of ordinary sandbox sand fill 1 teaspoon, then 76.8 million grains of sand will fill a 1-gallon container. At that rate, a sandbox 12 inches deep, covering the countries of Egypt, Israel, Lebanon, Syria, and Iraq, would hold as many grains of sand as there are stars in the universe. That's only 631,000 square miles, and there are many hundreds of thousands more miles of beaches than that on earth.

LASER RANGING (OR LIDAR)

Long distances can be measured by laser beams. Because we know the speed of light, we can measure distance to an object by the time it takes light to reach it and return. Laser beams from two far-distant observatories are sent up to the moon and bounced off a mirror left there by astronauts. The measurements tell the precise distance between the observatories. One thing scientists can learn from a series of these LIDAR measurements is how fast the continents are drifting apart.

HOW THE WORLD IS MEASURED

The Egyptians were the first people to divide a circle into 360 parts, or degrees. They drew the imaginary lines on earth that we call latitude and longitude. The easiest way to remember latitude and longitude is this:

Latitude: These are the lines that go around the earth, with the equator at 0 degrees. Think of latitude like a lateral pass in football—not up and high, but parallel to the ground. Imagine cutting the earth in half at the equator, and slicing it like an onion. There are 180 "slices" or lines, called parallels, that measure the distance from the North to the South Pole like this:

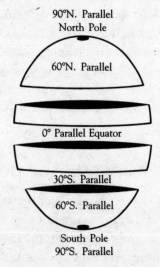

90°N. Parallel
North Pole

60°N. Parallel

0° Parallel Equator

30°S. Parallel
60°S. Parallel

South Pole
90°S. Parallel

Longitude slices the earth from north to south like sections of an orange in lines called meridians. Think of them as long =

longitude. They measure distance east and west in degrees like this:

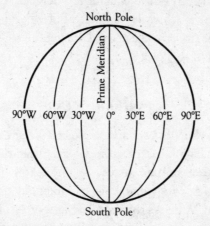

The Prime Meridian: This is the important longitude line, the one marked 0 degrees, where the measurements start for distance east and west. The prime meridian runs through the original site of the Royal Observatory, in Greenwich, England. Until 100 years ago, different countries ran the prime meridian through their own capital cities just because they felt like it. It has gone through Paris, Madrid, Cracow, Copenhagen, Rome, Augsburg, Beijing, St. Petersburg (Russia), and Washington, D.C.. Finally, at the International Meridian Conference in 1884, it was decided that the prime meridian would always be located in Greenwich, England, which certainly made it easier for everyone to figure .out where in the world they were.

Measuring East and West

The longitudes east of the prime meridian are numbered from 1 degree E to 179 degrees E. Longitudes west are numbered from 1 degree W to 179 degrees W. The International Date Line (see page 61) is the halfway mark at 180 degrees.

Measuring North and South

Latitude lines south of the equator are numbered from 1 degree S to 90 degrees S, which is the South Pole. Latitude lines north of the equator are marked from 1 degree N to 90 degrees N, which is the North Pole.

X Marks the Spot

Globe makers draw lines marking every 10 degrees of longitude and latitude. Each line of latitude is further divided into 60 minutes and each minute into 60 seconds. You can find a place on a map by knowing what lines of longitude and latitude run through it like "X marks the spot." That spot is called the *coordinate*. A coordinate is two numbers: the first is the latitude; it tells how far north of the equator that spot is. The second is longitude; it tells how far east or west of the prime meridian the place is. For example, if you wanted to find Greenwich, England, you'd look for 0 degree longitude, and you'd run your finger along that line north from the equator to the latitude marked 51 degrees, 28 minutes.

Can you find these places on your map or globe?
Disney World at latitude 28.28 N, and longitude 81.32 W
Hollywood at 34.06N, 118.21 W
Tasmania at 38.20 S, 146.30 E
Transylvania at 46.30 N, 22.35 E
Washington, D.C., at 38.53 N, 77.02 W
Moscow at 55.05 N, 38.50 E

What are the longitude and latitude lines where you live?
Latitude? _____ Longitude? _____

WHAT'S YOUR ADDRESS IN THE UNIVERSE?

You live in the galaxy called the **Milky Way**

In the **Solar System**

On the third planet from the sun, called **Earth**

On the North American continent

At the longitude of _____

At the latitude of _____

In the nation of _____
    (United States of America or Canada?)

In the state or province of _____

In the county of _____

In the township of _____

In the city, village, or town of _____

On the street or post office box _____

At the house or apartment building number _____

ALL AT SEA:
NAUTICAL MEASUREMENTS

Fathom = 6 feet. It comes from the Danish word *faedn*, which means outstretched arms. Six feet is just about the length of a man's outstretched arms.

Mark Twain: To find the depth of the water, a sailor used to drop a weighted, marked line or rope. On the Mississippi River riverboats, the sailor taking the depth or "sounding" would call

"Mark," and then the depth. For 2 fathoms, he'd shout, "Mark twain." Samuel Clemens was a river pilot before he became an author and used the name Mark Twain.

Cable Length = 100 fathoms, or 600 feet. It was the length of a ship's cable in the days of sailing ships. The U.S. navy measures a cable length as 720 feet.

League = 3 miles. To travel 20,000 leagues under the sea is to travel 60,000 miles, or more than twice around the world.

Nautical Mile = 6,076.097 feet, or 10 cables. It is based on the distance around the earth at the equator. Each degree of longitude at the equator is equal to 60 nautical miles.

Knot = 1 nautical mile per hour; a measure of speed on the water. This is an old measurement. Early ships used a "log line" to measure speed. A small log was tied to a rope to keep the rope afloat when it was tossed overboard and unreeled. Knots were tied in the rope about 47 feet apart. A sailor counted the number of knots that ran off the reel of line in 28 seconds, and that was the number of nautical miles per hour, or knots, that was the ship's speed. A ship traveling 20 knots, is going 20 nautical miles an hour.

Offshore Territorial Limit = 3 miles. It is the distance a cannon could be fired during the late 1700s. Each country owns the territory that extends 3 miles from its shores.

MEASURING ENERGY

Foot-Pound: A foot-pound is the energy needed to raise a 1-pound object 1 foot off the ground in 1 second.

Manpower is the amount of energy needed to lift 90 pounds 1 foot off the ground in 1 second.

Horsepower is the ability to lift 550 pounds 1 foot off the ground in 1 second. A 100 hp (horsepower) engine can work 100 times faster than a horse.

MEASURING HEAT

As the air gets hotter, the mercury inside a thermometer expands and rises at a constant speed.

Fahrenheit: The German physicist Gabriel Daniel Fahrenheit invented a scale for measuring heat and cold, based on the temperature at which water freezes and boils. On this scale, water freezes at 32 degrees F. and boils at 212 degrees F.

Celsius: A Swedish astronomer, Anders Celsius, devised a metric system of measuring heat and cold in the 1700s. It is also called Centigrade, which means 100 steps. On this scale, water freezes at 0 degrees C and boils at 100 degrees C.

Changing Celsius to Fahrenheit

You can use this formula to convert Celsius temperature to Fahrenheit:

$$F = 1.8 \times C + 32$$

For example, if the temperature is 20 degrees C, you first multiply the 20 × 1.8, which equals 36. Then add 32. 36 + 32 = 68. So when it's 20 degrees C, you know it's 68 degrees F.

Changing Fahrenheit to Celsius

This formula works for converting Fahrenheit to Celsius. Punch in the numbers on your calculator.

$$C = \frac{F - 32 \times 5}{9}$$

For example, the outside temperature is 50 degrees F, first subtract 32 from the 50, which equals 18. Then multiply that answer by 5.5 × 18 = 90. Divide 90 by 9, which equals 10. A temperature of 50 degrees F equals 10 degrees C.

Or You Can Just Look It Up on This Chart

Celsius	Fahrenheit
0	32
5	4
10	50
20	68
25	77
30	86
35	95
40	104
50	122
60	140
70	158
80	176
90	194
100	212

The Coldest: The lowest limit of cold that anyone knows is called absolute zero. It is −273 degrees Celsius, or −459 degrees Fahrenheit.

The Hottest: The hottest temperature may be the center of the sun, which could be as high as 40,000,000 degrees C, or about 720,000,000 degrees F.

Cricket Thermometer

If you're ever outdoors, nowhere near a thermometer, and you just have to know the temperature, you can listen to a cricket. If you count the number of chirps a cricket makes in 15 seconds, and add 37, you will have the temperature.

CALORIES

Grown men cringe and women cry when they think of calories! But why? Because calories make them fat . . . or so they think. Actually, calories only measure the amount of heat and energy we get from food. Officially, a calorie is the unit used to measure the amount of heat needed to raise the temperature of 1 gram of water 1 degree Celsius. Different foods produce more heat and energy than others. If we eat more calories than our bodies use up in energy, the extra food is stored as fat. Fifteen ounces of butter contain 3,000 calories. That would give you more than enough energy for a whole day. You'd have to eat 37 pounds of lettuce to get the same number of calories. It's better to take calories from lots of different kinds of food, and work off any extra calories by exercising.

Burn off the Calories in One Hour

One hour of this	Uses this many calories
Watching TV	60
Sleeping	80
Playing Monopoly	150
Walking (3 miles an hour)	210
Playing Ping-Pong	220
Mowing the lawn (with a power mower)	250

One hour of this	Uses this many calories
Swimming	300
Horseback riding	350
Pitching a baseball	360
Riding a bike (5.5 mph)	380
Playing tennis	420
Playing basketball	500
Skiing (10 mph)	600
Running (10 mph)	900

How Many Calories in Your Favorite Snack?

Pepperoni pizza (1 slice) =	306 calories
Potato chips (1 ounce) =	150
Doritos, corn tortilla chips (1 ounce) =	140
Chocolate cookie (1) =	59
Hostess Twinkie (1) =	144
Peanut butter (1 tablespoon) =	86
Chocolate cake (1 slice) =	350
Cola (12 ounces) =	150
Hamburger =	275
Hot dog =	214
French fries =	274

The calorie number listed for the hamburger, hot dog, and french fries is an average of those made at fast-food restaurants.

How many miles would you have to ride your bike in order to work off the calories from an extra slice of pizza?

MEASURING LIGHT

Light travels in waves. It is measured from one wave peak to the next, like this:

More than 300 years ago, Isaac Newton found that light going through a prism breaks up into the colors of the rainbow. White light is made up of all the colors from red to violet. Red light travels in the longest wavelength, and violet has the shortest wavelength.

Ultraviolet Light is light the human eye cannot see because it is beyond the short waves of violet. Ultraviolet is the kind of lightwave that gives you a tan even on a cloudy day.

Infrared Light is made up of lightwaves longer than red lightwaves. We can't see this either. Infrared light is used in heat lamps. It's the kind of light used to make the binoculars that allow soldiers to "see" a dark battlefield at night.

Nanometer: Light is measured by the nanometer, which is one-billionth of a meter.

Electric Eyes: Lightwaves can be turned into electrical energy. Engineers use lightwaves to make the "electric eyes" that open doors so magically when you walk into a store.

Candlepower is the measure of brightness. It is expressed in terms of the brightness given off by the flame of a candle of a certain type and size. A lighthouse uses more than 6 million candlepower.

MEASURING SOUND

Sound travels in waves that vibrate. The speed of sound depends on what it is traveling through. At sea level, at 32 degrees F, sound travels 760 miles per hour through the air. But it travels through water at 3,204 miles an hour, and through a steel beam at 11,181 miles an hour. Mach I is the speed of sound. Mach II is twice the speed of sound. The measurement is named for Ernst Mach, an Austrian physicist who studied sound waves about 100 years ago.

If a pilot flies at Mach I, he is not necessarily flying at 760 miles an hour. At a high altitude, a pilot could be flying 600 miles an hour and still be at Mach I because sound travels more slowly through the thinner air at higher levels.

The Flash and Then the Noise

We see lightning before we hear it because light travels 800,000 times faster than sound. Lightning moves at 50,000 miles a second. That is fast enough to heat the air to 50,000 degrees. We can see it many miles away because each yard of air the lightning zaps through gets so hot that it shines as bright as 1 million 100 watt light bulbs.

Supersonic aircraft fly faster than the speed of sound (*super* = more than; *sonic* = sound).

Pitch is how high or low the tones sound. High-pitched tones are made by waves vibrating fast and close together. Low-pitched sounds are made by waves vibrating slowly. If you stretch a thin rubber band as far as it will go, and twang it, the short, fast vibrations make a high-pitched sound. But if you twang a thick, fat, loosely stretched rubber band, the slow, relaxed vibrations make a low-pitched sound.

Hertz is the number of sound waves per second. It measures the frequency of vibrations. The lowest note on a piano sends out sound waves at 27 hertz (Hz). The highest note sends out waves at the rate of 4,000 Hz.

Infrasonic: Humans can hear sound down to about 20 hertz. Sounds slower than 20 hertz are too low for humans to hear, and they are called infrasonic. (*Infra* means below, and *sonic* means sound.) Elephants and whales send long distance infrasonic signals. We can't hear them, but scientists have picked up the messages on equipment that changes it to messages we can hear.

Ultrasonic: Sounds above 20,000 hertz are too high for humans to hear, and these are called ultrasonic. (*Ultra* means above.) Bats and dolphins send ultrasonic signals, which have been recorded and slowed down to a level we can hear. The "silent" dog whistles are silent only to us; dogs can hear the higher sound.

- Humans hear 20 to 20,000 hertz
- Dogs hear 15 to 50,000 hertz
- Cats hear 60 to 65,000 hertz

- Bats hear 1,000 to 120,000 hertz
- Dolphins hear 150 to 150,000 hertz

Decibels: A decibel is the comparison of one sound to another on a scale of 0 to 150. Zero is the softest sound any human can hear. Here are some decibel comparisons:

- Leaves rustling: 10 decibels
- A soft whisper heard from 16 feet away: 30 decibels
- Average conversation, 3 feet away: 60 decibels
- Heavy traffic or chain saw, at 50 feet: 100 decibels
- Amplified rock music: 110 decibels
- Jet aircraft at takeoff, 200 feet away: 120 decibels
- Air raid siren: 130 decibels (painful for humans)
- Jet takeoff, 100 feet away: 140 to 150 decibels

Big League Noise

One of the secret weapons of the Buffalo Bills football team is its fans. They make so much noise that the other team can't hear its own signals. At the January 1992 Eastern Championship game against the Denver Broncos in the Buffalo stadium, the noise level at some moments was as loud as a jet taking off—120 decibels.

CLOTH MEASURES

Bolt = 120 yards of cloth.

Skein = 360 feet of yarn.

Hank = 560 yards of wool, or 840 yards of cotton.

Heer = 600 yards of wool yarn.

Iron = 0.02 inches, the measure of leather in the sole of a shoe.

Line = 0.025, a measure of buttons.

Other Odd Measures

Score: A group of 20. If you live four score years, you will be eighty, or four groups of twenty years.

Baker's Dozen: 13 items. In England in the 1600s, bakers were ordered to make rolls smaller in order to save flour. Customers got angry, so bakers kept them happy by adding an extra roll to every dozen.

Hogshead: 63 gallons. It's a measure of liquid in a cask or barrel.

As the Crow Flies: This old saying isn't a real measurement, of course, but it refers to the fact that the shortest distance between two places is a straight line. It assumes that crows fly straight to where they want to go without any detours or doubling back.

Board Foot: A measure of lumber. A board foot is 1 foot long, 1 foot wide, and 1 inch thick.

Quire: A measure of paper = 24 sheets.

Ream: A measure of paper = 500 sheets.

Cord: A stack of wood that measures 8 feet long by 4 feet wide by 4 feet high. If you buy a **cord foot** of wood, you are getting a stack 4 feet high, 4 feet long, and 1 foot long.

INSTRUMENTS THAT MEASURE

Sextant: Sailors use the sextant to navigate by locating the ship's position of latitude and longitude. They can measure the distance by sighting the North Star at night, or the sun during the day, and reading the angles that tell them the position of longitude and latitude.

Surveyor's Chain: Measures short distances. Each link in the chain is 7.92 inches long, and the whole chain is 66 inches. When the Greeks first surveyed their coastline in 300 B.C., they used a rope as a measuring tape. It was knotted at regular intervals, and it could float in case it fell in the ocean.

Geiger Counter: An instrument for detecting radiation.

Spirometer: Measures the amount of air in the lungs.

Orometer: Measures the height of mountains. It is used by mountain climbers and map makers.

Konometer: Measures the amount of dust and pollen in the air.

Pyrheliometer: Measures the sun's heat.

Astrophometer: Measures the brightness of a star's light.

Oometer: Measures the size of birds' eggs.

Galactometer: Measures the flow of milk.

Craniometer: Measures the size of a skull.

Pedometer: Measures the distance a person walks.

HOW CAN YOU MEASURE IF YOU DON'T HAVE A RULER? LET ME COUNT THE WAYS

Suppose you have to measure something, but you have no ruler, no tape measure, or yardstick? What can you use? Your shoelaces, for one thing. For example, suppose you want to measure the distance from your house to your friend's house. Take out one shoelace, and use it as though it's a ruler. Measure the number of shoelace lengths between the two houses. When you get home, measure the shoelace. Multiply the length of the shoelace by the number of "ruler" laces. Suppose you have measured 200 shoelaces between houses, and your shoelace is 24 inches long, or two feet. Multiplying 2 feet by 200 equals 400 feet from your house to your friend's.

What else could you use? Try a sheet of typing paper, which measures 8½ inches by 11 inches. Use the 11 inch side for easier multiplying. Or use an new unsharpened pencil, which is 8½ inches long. Or use a quarter. The diameter of a quarter is just about 1 inch.

What other things can you think of to measure with?

Measure by Smoots?

The Massachusetts Avenue Bridge in Cambridge, Massachusetts, usually called Harvard Bridge, is measured in smoots. In the fall of 1958, Oliver R. Smoot, Jr., wanted to join Lambda Chi Alpha fraternity at the Massachusetts Institute of Technology (MIT). Hopeful members are called pledges, and fraternity members can ask pledges to do most anything. Oliver Smoot, Jr., was asked to measure Harvard Bridge with his body. With the help of other pledges, who turned Smoot end to end, the bridge was found to be 364.4 smoots and one ear long. The stunt has become a tradition at MIT, and twice a year the smoot marks are touched up. When city workers repaired the bridge, they carefully repainted the smoot marks.

Numbers in

CHAPTER FIVE

Sports and Games

Without numbers, sports wouldn't be much fun. How would you score a tennis match or a football game? How would we count the number of players needed on a basketball team or a baseball team? How would anyone measure the size of a playing field?

FOOTBALL

Football began in 1875 when the colleges of Harvard and Yale agreed on a set of rules for a new game that used parts of English rugby and parts of an American game that was a lot like soccer. This is what they decided:

Number of Players: Two teams of eleven players each.

Size of Field: 160 feet wide; 360 feet long, with two end zones each 30 feet long.

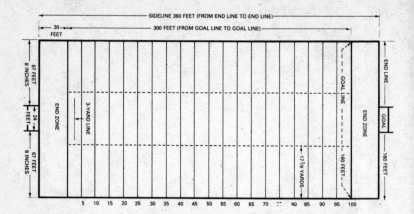

Goalposts: The two posts are 18 feet, 4 inches apart, and the crossbar is 10 feet above the ground.

Size of Ball: An oval ball (officially called a prolate spheroid) that weighs 14 to 15 ounces; it is 28 to 28½ inches long, and 21 inches around its widest part.

Scoring: a touchdown = 6 points
an extra point, kicked after a touchdown = 1 point
(also called a conversion)
a field goal = 3 points
a safety = 2 points

Time: The game is divided into four quarters, each lasting 15 minutes, with 2-minute intermissions between quarters, and 20 minutes at halftime.

National Football League (NFL) Records

- *Most points in a career:* 2,002 points; scored by George Blanda, Chicago Bears.
- *Most touchdown passes in a season:* 48; scored by Dan Marino, Miami Dolphins, 1984.

- *Most rushing yards in a season:* 2,105; scored by Eric Dickerson, Los Angeles Rams, 1984.
- *Longest field goal:* 63 yards; kicked by Tom Dempsey, New Orleans Saints, in a game against the Detroit Lions, November 8, 1970.
- *Most passes completed in a career:* 3,686; by Fran Tarkenton.

BASKETBALL

Dr. James Naismith invented basketball in 1891, when he was a physical education instructor at the YMCA in Springfield, Massachusetts. He was looking for an active but not too rough sport to play indoors in the winter. The first basketball game was played with a soccer ball and two peach baskets hung up at either end of a gym.

Number of Players: Two teams of five players, made up of two forwards, two guards, and one center.

Size of Court: 50 feet wide by 84 to 94 feet long.

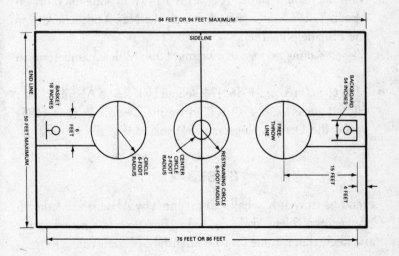

Freethrow Line to Backboard: 15 feet.

Floor to Rim of Basket: 10 feet.

Diameter of Basket: 18 inches at the rim.

Size of Ball: 29½ to 30 inches around, weighing 20 to 22 ounces. When dropped from a height of 6 feet, the ball should bounce back 49 to 54 inches.

Scoring: a field goal, or basket = 2 points
a freethrow = 1 point
a shot from more that 30 feet = 3 points (in the American Basketball Association)

Time: Four quarters of 12 minutes each.

National Basketball Records

- *Most points in a game:* 100; scored by Wilt Chamberlain on March 2, 1962, in a game between the New York Knicks and the Philadelphia 76ers.
- *Highest scoring average in a season:* 50.4; Wilt Chamberlain in 1962.
- *Most points in a career:* 36,474; scored by Kareem Abdul-Jabbar.
- *Highest game total:* 370; scored by the Detroit Pistons (186) versus the Denver Nuggets (184) in 1983.

BASEBALL

Legend has it that baseball was invented by Abner Doubleday in Cooperstown, New York, in 1839. But experts agree that it's more likely that it came from an English boys' game called Rounders. Rounders had four "stones" forming a square and a "feeder" who threw the ball to a "striker" who tried to hit it.

Number of Players: Nine on each of two teams.

Size of Field: A 90-foot square called a diamond.

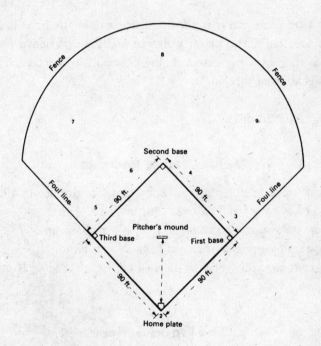

Pitcher's Mound: 10 inches high, 18 feet in diameter.

Pitcher's Plate: Called a rubber; 2 feet by 6 inches.

Home Plate: 17 inches on the longest side, with the end pointed to fit into the diamond.

Bases: Each a 15-inch square.

Pitcher's Plate to Home Plate: 60 feet 6 inches.

Catcher's Box: 8 feet by 43 inches.

Size of Ball: Weighs 5 to 5½ ounces; 9 to 9¼ inches around.

Scoring: Each player is allowed three strikes, then he is out. After four balls, the player walks to first base. When a player rounds the bases and gets to home plate, a run is scored. Each team is allowed three outs.

Time: Nine innings.

Major League Records

- *Most runs batted in a game*: 12; by James Bottomley in 1924.
- *Most home runs in a lifetime*: 755; by Hank Aaron.
- *Most strikeouts in a season*: 383; by Nolan Ryan in 1973.
- *Most no-hit games in a career*: 6; by Nolan Ryan.
- *Best pitching year*: 1984 for Rick Sutcliffe with .941%; 16 wins, 1 loss.

The World Series

The World Series decides the baseball championship. The first one was played in 1903. Originally the winner was the team that took the best of nine games. Now seven games are played; the winner must take four. There are twenty-six major league teams divided into two leagues: American League, that has won forty-eight World Series, and the National League, that has won thirty-six World Series.

The New York Yankees have played in the Series thirty-three times and won twenty-two. One pitcher has thrown a perfect game in a World Series—Don Larsen, the New York Yankees versus the Brooklyn Dodgers on October 8, 1956.

HOCKEY

Hockey probably came from an old Dutch sport called *kolf* that was played on ice with a ball and a crooked stick. In 1855, an army unit called the Royal Canadian Rifles in Kingston, Ontario, started to play hockey, and by 1880, the game had spread into the northern United States. The Canadian Hockey Hall of Fame is located in Kingston, Ontario.

Number of Players: Six on each of two teams.

Size of Ice Rink: 85 feet by 200 feet.

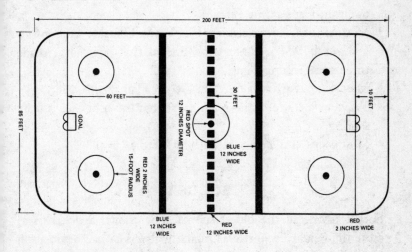

Size of Goal: 4 feet high, 6 feet wide, and 2 to 3 feet deep.

Size of Face-off Circles: 20 feet in diameter, with a 12-inch center circle.

Puck: 3 inches in diameter, 1 inch thick, weighs 6 ounces, and is made of rubber.

Size of Stick: The handle can be no longer than 4 feet, 5 inches; the blade 3 inches wide and no longer than 1 foot, 2½ inches; the goalie's stick can be no wider than 3½ inches.

Scoring: Each goal is worth one point.

Time: Three periods of 20 minutes each, with 10-minute breaks in between.

National Hockey League Records

- *Most points in one season:* 215; scored by Wayne Gretzky, Edmonton, Canada, in 1986.
- *Most hat tricks of the season:* 10; Wayne Gretzky, Edmonton, 1982 and 1984. A "hat trick" means that one player made three goals in one game.
- *Most shutouts in a season:* 22; by George Hainsworth, Montreal, 1929. In a shutout one team prevented the other team from scoring.
- *Most points in a lifetime:* 1,850; by Gordie Howe.

SOCCER

Soccer is one of the oldest sports. It is known as football in more than eighty countries. Originally it was called "association football" to distinguish it from rugby. People shortened that to "assoc football," which they pronounced as "A-sock," and by 1863, that had become "soccer."

Number of Players: Two teams of eleven players each.

Size of Field: 50 to 100 yards wide by 100 to 130 yards long.

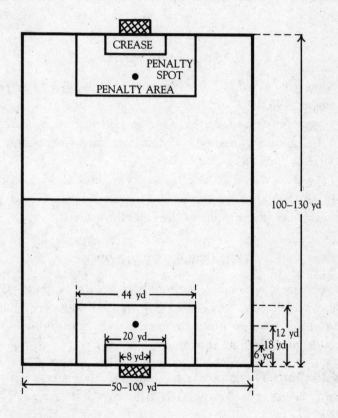

Size of Goal: 8 feet high and 8 yards wide.

Center Circle: 20 yards in diameter.

Size of Ball: 27 to 28 inches around; weighs 14 to 18 ounces; made up of thirty-two panels. (The more panels in a ball, the more perfectly round it is.)

Scoring: Each goal is worth one point.

Time: Two 45-minute periods, with 10-minute rests between periods.

Soccer Records

- *Most goals scored in a first class match:* 16; scored by Stephan Stanis, 1942.
- *Longest time a goalie prevented any goals in international matches:* 1,142 minutes; Goalie Dino Zoff from Italy, from September 1972 to June 1974.
- *Longest time heading a ball:* 5 hours, 3 minutes, and 18 seconds, nonstop by Mikael Palmquist, Sweden, 1988. ("Heading" means the player bounces the ball off his head.)

THE LONGEST GAMES

Baseball: A minor league game between the Rochester Red Wings and the Pawtucket Red Sox in 1981 was stopped after thirty-three innings with a tie score of 2-2. It was finished two months later. Pawtucket won, 3-2.

Basketball: The longest game lasted 120 hours between two teams playing at S. Towne Mall in Sandy, Utah, August 22 to 27, 1988.

Boxing Match: 110 rounds between Andy Bowen and Jack Burke of New Orleans, April 6 and 7, 1893. After 7 hours and 19 minutes, it was declared "no contest" and neither boxer won.

Tennis Match: The longest singles match lasted 145 hours, 44 minutes, played by Bobby McWaters and Ed VanTregt at Kingston Plantation, Myrtle Beach, South Carolina, September 25 to October 1, 1988.

Hockey: The Detroit Red Wings and the Montreal Maroons played for 2 hours, 56 minutes, and 30 seconds in 1936. A normal game lasts 1 hour and 20 minutes. The final score was 1-0 after the sixth period of overtime. They played at the Forum in Montreal, March 25, 1936. The Red Wings goalie, Norm Smith, kept ninety-two shots from entering the goal.

BOWLING

Bowling with nine pins was an old German game, which settlers brought to the new colonies being settled in America in the 1700s. In the 1840s, the game of nine-pins was closed down in some states because people were betting, and criminals were hanging around the bowling alleys. So one clever bowling alley owner decided to add a pin. A game of ten-pins wasn't illegal, and bowling has used ten pins ever since.

THE OLYMPIC GAMES

The Olympic Games began in Greece in 776 B.C. as part of a five-day religious celebration, and they continued for 1,100 years. In 393 A.D., the Roman emperor Theodosius I stopped the games, and they didn't start again until 1896. In that year, 311 men from thirteen nations competed. The Olympics have been played every four years since, except during World War I and World War II. Today 10,000 men and women from more than 100 nations compete in 237 different events.

A Long Old Race

The first Olympic marathon race was run at the first modern games in Greece in 1896. It was held in honor of an ancient journey made in 490 B.C. by a Greek messenger named Pheidippedes. He had completed an astonishing two-day run of 150 miles from the city of Athens to Sparta to get help for the Athenian army. Two days later he ran from the Plain of Marathon to Athens to spread the news that the Greeks had defeated Persia in a war. After 22 miles without stopping, he arrived at the city, shouted, "Rejoice, we conquer!" collapsed, and died.

The official distance for a marathon wasn't set officially at 26 miles, 385 yards until 1924. The odd distance had first been run in 1908 at the London Games. The marathon course was laid out between Windsor Castle and the White City stadium, a distance of 26 miles. But the organizers wanted the runners to finish the race in front of the royal box where King Edward VII could see it. That added the extra 385 yards. Since then the word *marathon* has often been used to describe other long, difficult tasks.

Go for the Gold

In 1972, swimmer Mark Spitz won seven gold medals at the Olympic Games in Munich, Germany. It was a world record for the number of gold medals won by one person in one year. The Olympic gold medals aren't solid gold—they are silver, coated with gold.

Olympic Sports That Are Judged

A race is won by the clock, but sports not based on speed must be judged. The judges watch each competitor and then hold up a card with the number of the score they awarded. The highest and lowest scores are thrown out, and the remaining scores are averaged to get the final score. Diving is based on a scale of 0 to 10, with seven judges. Gymnastics also uses a 0-10 scale, but has four judges. Figure skating is based on 0-6 and has nine judges.

The First Perfect Scores

- In the 1976 Olympic Games, fourteen-year-old Nadia Comaneci from Rumania was awarded a perfect ten score in gymnastics. Before the Games were over, she had won seven perfect tens.

- In 1972, all seven judges gave Michael Finneran a score of ten during the Olympic diving trials in Chicago. It was the first perfect score in diving.

- In figure skating, all nine judges gave the first perfect score of 6.0 to Jayne Torvil and Christopher Dean for their artistic presentation in free dance competition at the 1983 World Championships in Helsinki, Finland.

The Combination Competitions

Biathlon: Two events in one competition. A cross country ski race is combined with rifle shooting. It was started in the Scandinavian countries for military training and for hunting.

Triathlon: Three events in one competition; started in 1978. Contestants swim 2.4 miles in the ocean, followed immediately by a 112-mile bicycle race, followed by a 26-mile, 385-yard marathon run, with no time out between events.

Pentathlon: Five events in five days. It began as military training.

Day one: 1,000 miles cross country horseback riding and jump-
ing
Day two: Round-robin fencing event
Day three: Pistol shooting
Day four: 300-meter freestyle swim
Day five: 4,000-meter cross country run

Decathlon: One event involving ten track and field events in
two days.

Event one: 100-yard dash
Event two: 440-yard dash
Event three: 1-mile run
Event four: 110-yard high
hurdles
Event five: Shot put

Event six: Discus throw
Event seven: Javelin throw
Event eight: Long jump
Event nine: High jump
Event ten: Pole vault

WHAT CAN BE DONE IN AN HOUR?

- If you were Annie Lambrechts of Belgium, you could roller
skate 23 miles in an hour, as she did in 1985.
- If you were Robert Commers of Pennsylvania, you could jump
rope 13,783 revolutions with no faults in an hour, as he did
in 1989.
- If you were Francesco Moser of Italy, you could bicycle 31
miles and 1,381 yards in Mexico City, where the altitude
makes exercise tougher, as he did in 1984.

THE NEED-FOR-SPEED RECORDS

Roller Skating: Top speed of 31.07 miles per hour, set by L.
Antoniel of Italy in 1987.

Downhill Skiing: 124.412 miles per hour; set by Steve McKinney in 1978.

Skateboarding: 71.79 miles an hour; set by Richard Brown in, 1979.

Running: Over 25 miles an hour; set by Carl Lewis in 1984 Olympic sprint relay.

SPEEDY NUMBERS

- *Fastest baseball:* 100.9 miles per hour; thrown by Nolan Ryan on August 20, 1974, in California.
- *Fastest hockey puck:* 118.3 miles per hour; shot by Bobby Hull.
- *Fastest tennis serve:* 163.6 miles per hour; hit by William Tilden in 1931. With modern measuring equipment, today's tennis record stands at 138 miles per hour by Steven Denton in 1984.
- *Fastest frisbee:* 74 miles an hour; thrown by Alan Bonopane and caught by Tim Selinske in California in 1980.
- *Fastest golf ball:* Can be driven off a tee at 170 miles an hour.
- *Fastest ball in any game:* The jai-alai ball, which travels up to 188 miles an hour.

FIVE LONG, THIN SPORTS

Bowling: The alley measures 78 feet long and only 41 to 42 inches wide.

Curling: The rink is 138 feet long and 14 feet wide.

Shuffleboard: The court measures 52 feet by 6 feet.

Horseshoe Pitching: The court is 50 feet long, and 10 feet wide. The stakes are placed 40 feet apart for men, and 30 feet apart for women.

Lawn Bowling: The court is 120 feet long and 20 feet wide.

UNUSUAL SCORING TERMS

Love: In tennis, love means zero. It comes from the French word *l'oeuf*, which means egg. Probably "egg" was their slang word for zero, as in, "That's 15 for me, an egg for you." When the game was taken up in England, the French word was pronounced "luff," which became "love."

Par: In golf, the average number of shots it takes to get the ball in the hole.

Eagle: In golf, two strokes under par, or two strokes less than par, which is average for that hole.

Birdie: In golf, one stroke under par.

Bogie: In golf, one stroke over par.

Dutch 200: In bowling, a 200 game score made by alternating spares with strikes.

Safety: In football, two points scored by the defense when the offensive team gets caught behind their own goal line with the ball.

Ringer: In horseshoe pitching, when a player circles the stake with a horseshoe, worth 3 points.

Try: In rugby, grounding the ball in the opponent's end zone. In union or amateur play, a try is worth 4 points; in league or professional play, it's worth 3.

Turkey: In bowling, three strikes in a row.

Hat Trick: In hockey, scoring three goals in one game—from the old tradition of rewarding the player with a hat.

HOW THINGS MEASURE UP

- *Largest roller rink:* 68,000 square feet; in London, England.
- *Largest stadium:* Strahov Stadium in Prague, Czechoslovakia, which seats 240,000.
- *Largest bowling center:* 144 lanes; in Osaka, Japan.
- *Largest swimming pool:* Orthlieb Pool in Morocco, a salt water pool that covers 8.9 acres, and measures 1,574 feet by 75 feet.
- *Largest kind of playing field:* A polo court, which covers 12.4 acres. It is 300 yards long and 200 yards wide.
- *Smallest kind of playing field:* The table used for table tennis. It is 9 feet long and 5 feet wide.

BALLS, SHOTS, AND STONES: HOW THEY MEASURE UP

Cage Ball: The biggest ball made; some are larger than 6 feet in diameter. Also known as the earth ball, it is used in physical education classes in a game in which one team tries to push this enormous ball into the other team's end zone.

Bowling Ball: No more than 27 inches around, and between 10 to 16 pounds. A standard bowling ball for a child weighs six pounds.

Curling Stone: No more than 36 inches around and 4.5 inches high; weighs 42.5 pounds.

Field Hockey Ball: 8.75 to 9.25 inches around; weighs 5.5 to 5.75 ounces.

Golf Ball: No more than 1.68 inches in diameter; weighs no more than 1.62 ounces.

Polo Ball: Diameter of 3.25 inches; weighs 4.5 ounces.

Table Tennis: Less than one-tenth of an ounce.

Tennis Ball: Diameter of 2.5 inches; weighs 2 ounces. For the best bounce, tennis balls should be kept refrigerated at 68 degrees F.

Waterpolo Ball: Similar to a soccer ball: 27 to 28 inches around; weighs 14 to 16 ounces.

Shot Put: The men's shot weighs 16 pounds; the women's weighs 8 pounds, 13 ounces.

SEVENTH INNING STRETCH

Baseball fans stand up to stretch during the seventh inning. In June 1882, in a tight game between two small colleges, one coach had everyone stand up before the seventh inning as a way of breaking the tension. The stretch was first introduced in a professional game at the World Series between the New York Giants and Brooklyn in October 1889.

BASEBALL SQUARE OR DIAMOND?

A baseball field is a square. When the game started almost 150 years ago, town teams had their own rules. In some places the batter stood halfway between home plate and first base. From that position, the field looked like a square. Members of the Knickerbocker Baseball Club in New York wrote down rules for baseball in 1845, and one of the rules said that the batter must stand at home plate. That's where batters always stand now, and from that spot, the baseball field is a diamond.

HOW DO YOU FIGURE A BATTING AVERAGE?

A player's batting average measures the number of hits a player would get if he were to bat 1,000 times. Anything over .300 is excellent. If a player gets 71 hits out of 253 times at bat, his batting average would be figured like this: divide 71 by 253 = .2806324. Usually the average is rounded out to three decimal places, but sometimes it's important to work it out to four decimal places.

In 1949, Ted Williams, playing for Boston, and George Kell, playing for Detroit, both had batting averages of .343. To break the tie for the American League batting championship, their batting averages were worked out to the fourth decimal. Williams had .3427, but Kell's hits averaged out to .3429. Kell won the honor because his average was .0002 of a point higher.

WHAT'S AN ERA?

ERA means Earned Run Average. It's an important number for a pitcher. It tells how many earned runs a pitcher allows for every nine innings he pitches. Runs scored because of a pitcher's or a fielder's error don't count as earned runs.

- *An ERA is figured like this:* Suppose a pitcher allowed sixty runs in two hundred innings.

  Step 1: On your calculator punch in the number of runs: 60.

  Step 2: Now multiply the number of runs by 9, the number of innings in a game: 60 × 9 = 540.

  Step 3: Divide 540 by the number of innings pitched: 540 divided by 200 = 2.70. The ERA for that pitcher is 2.70, which means he allowed fewer than three runs for every nine innings he pitched. He is a good pitcher!

BASEBALL MUD MEANS MONEY

Every major league team scours their new baseballs with mud before a game, and they all use the same mud! They use Lena Blackburne's Baseball Rubbing Mud. No one knows exactly

where it comes from because the Blackburne family guards the secret very well. They go out in rowboats at night to "harvest" the mud from a riverbottom somewhere near the Delaware River in southern New Jersey. After they sift the mud, they sell it for $75 a can.

SEVENTEEN RETIRED BASEBALL NUMBERS: AND THE PLAYERS WHO WORE THEM

To honor a player who has given outstanding service to the team, in playing and in leadership, his number is retired when he retires. These are some of the numbers that will never be worn by another man playing on that team:

#4 Lou Gehrig, New York Yankees
#5 Joe DiMaggio, New York Yankees
#5 Johnny Bench, Cincinnati Reds
#6 Stan Musial, St. Louis Cardinals
#6 Steve Garvey, San Diego Padres
#7 Mickey Mantle, New York Yankees
#8 Carl Yastrzemski, Boston Red Sox
#8 Yogi Berra, New York Yankees
#9 Ted Williams, Boston Red Sox
#20 Frank Robinson, Cincinnati Reds and Baltimore Orioles
#22 Jim Palmer, Baltimore Orioles
#24 Willie Mays, San Francisco Giants
#29 Rod Carew, Minnesota Twins and California Angels
#39 Roy Campanella, Los Angeles Dodgers
#41 Tom Seaver, New York Mets
#42 Jackie Robinson, Los Angeles Dodgers
#44 Hank Aaron, Milwaukee Brewers and Atlanta Braves

The New York Yankees have retired twelve numbers, the most in the major leagues. Only three players have had their numbers retired by more than one team: Hank Aaron (44), Rod Carew (29), and Frank Robinson (20).

TEN FAMOUS RETIRED BASKETBALL NUMBERS: AND THE PLAYERS WHO WORE THEM

#1 Oscar Robertson, Milwaukee Bucks
#2 Red Auerbach, Boston Celtics
#6 Bill Russell, Boston Celtics
#7 Pete Maravich, Utah Jazz
#10 Walt Frazier, New York Knicks
#13 Wilt Chamberlain, Los Angeles Lakers and Philadelphia 76ers
#17 John Havlicek, Boston Celtics
#32 Julius Erving, New Jersey Nets
#44 Jerry West, Los Angeles Lakers
#23 "Magic" Johnson, Los Angeles Lakers

The Boston Celtics have retired fifteen uniform numbers, more than any other team. Four players have had their numbers retired by more than one team:

Julius Erving—32 by New Jersey Nets and 6 by Philadelphia 76ers
Oscar Robertson—14 by Sacramento Kings and 1 by Milwaukee Bucks
Nate Thurmond—42 by Golden State Warriors and Cleveland Cavaliers
Wilt Chamberlain—13 by Los Angeles Lakers and Philadelphia 76ers

THIRTEEN RETIRED FOOTBALL NUMBERS: AND THE PLAYERS WHO WORE THEM

#10 Fran Tarkenton, Minnesota Vikings
#12 Bob Griese, Miami Dolphins
#12 Joe Namath, New York Jets
#14 Dan Fouts, San Diego Chargers
#15 Bart Starr, Green Bay Packers
#19 Johnny Unitas, Indianapolis Colts
#32 Jim Brown, Cleveland Browns
#34 Walter Payton, Chicago Bears
#34 Earl Campbell, Houston Oilers
#70 Art Donovan, Indianapolis Colts
#74 Merlin Olsen, Los Angeles Rams
#77 Red Grange, Chicago Bears
#87 Dwight Clark, San Francisco 49ers

The Chicago Bears have retired ten numbers, the most for any team. The New York Giants, Indianapolis Colts, and San Francisco 49ers have each retired seven numbers. No football player has had his number retired from more than one team.

TEN RETIRED HOCKEY NUMBERS: AND THE PLAYERS WHO WORE THEM

#2 Tim Horton, Buffalo Sabres
#4 Bobby Orr, Boston Bruins
#7 nPhil Esposito, Boston Bruins
#8 Marc Tardif, Quebec Nordiques
#9 Bobby Hull, Chicago Black Hawks and Winnipeg Jets
#9 Gordie Howe, Detroit Red Wings and Hartford Whalers
#10 Guy Lafleur, Montreal Canadiens
#11 Wany Maki, Vancouver Canucks

#16 Bobby Clarke, Philadelphia Flyers
#35 Tony Esposito, Chicago Black Hawks

Seven uniform numbers have been retired by the Boston Bruins. The Montreal Canadiens have retired six. Two players have had their numbers retired from two different teams: Bobby Hull and Gordie Howe.

ONE TO TEN IN SPORTS

One-on-One: One person plays against another. Challenging your dad to basketball in the backyard is a one-on-one game.

One in the Dark: In bowling, "one in the dark" is a pin left standing behind another pin, where you can't see it.

One-Two Punch: In boxing, this is a fast left punch followed by a quick right punch.

Two-Bagger: Running two bases in baseball.

Two-Minute Warning: In football, the referee warns the two teams when they have only two minutes left in the half.

Three-Second Rule: In basketball, an offensive player can't be in the free-throw lane for more than 3 seconds while his team has the ball.

Three-Point Stance: This is the position of two feet and one hand on the ground, which a football lineman takes before the ball is snapped.

Four-Bagger: A home run in baseball.

Four-Waller: A person who plays four-wall handball.

Foursome: Four players are standard in tournament golf.

Five: A basketball team.

Five-Man Line: A defensive lineup in football, with two ends, two tackles, and one middle guard.

Sixth Man: In basketball, the sixth man is the player used regularly as the first substitute. He is equally as important as a first-string player.

Six: A hockey team.

Eight: An eight-oared racing shell.

Eight Ball: A game of billiards.

Nine: A baseball team.

Front Nine and Back Nine: The first nine holes on a golf course, and the last nine holes of an eighteen-hole course.

Ten-Finger Grip: The right way to hold a golf club.

Ten Count: In boxing, the referee gives a boxer to the count of ten to get up after he has been knocked down.

THE NUMBERS ON GOLF CLUBS

The number of the golf club tells a golfer the kind of shot to use it for. A high number means that the ball will go high and short because the head of the club is at a sharp angle. You'd use a high-numbered club to chop a ball out of the rough, for example. A low number means that the ball will go long because the head of the club is straighter.

1 wood, driver	1 iron, driving iron
2 wood, brassie	2 iron, midiron
3 wood, spoon	3 iron, mid mashie
4 wood, cleek	4 iron, mashie iron
5 wood, baffy	5 iron, mashie
	6 iron, spade mashie
	7 iron, mashie niblick
	8 iron, pitching niblick
	9 iron, niblick

DID YOU KNOW THAT . . .

- There are over 400 dimples on a golf ball.
- There are 108 stitches in a baseball.
- Every major league baseball team buys about 18,000 balls a season.
- Before each major league game, 144 baseballs are rubbed with mud which raises the grain of the leather, making it easier to grip.
- In the major leagues, the average baseball lasts about five pitches.
- Professional football teams use over 300 miles of adhesive tape in one season.
- Over 35 miles of woolen yarn are needed to cover a billard table measuring 12.5 feet by 6 feet 7 inches.
- In football there are no rules about uniform numbers, but the number 34 is most often worn by a running back, and kickers wear low numbers.

- A baseball can be made to curve 6½ inches from its normal course.
- In a year, 25 million tennis balls are used all over the world.

LONG RACES

Iditarod Dogsled Race: This is a 1,158 mile race from Auch to Nome, Alaska. It was named after an abandoned mining town on the old frozen mail route it follows. The Iditarod is held to commemorate an emergency dogsled mission to get medical supplies to the town during a diphteria epidemic in 1925.

Tour de France: The course for this bicycle race winds over 3,000 miles of roads through French countryside and towns. Hundreds of riders compete in the grueling twenty-three-day event.

Grand Prix: The most famous Grand Prix is the twenty-four-hour endurance car race held in Le Mans, France, over a 3,314.222-mile course.

Indy 500: Since May 30, 1911, a 500-mile car race has been held every year at the Indianapolis track. The cars go around the track two hundred times. Bobby Rahal holds the record for the fastest time—2 hours, 55 minutes, and 42.48 seconds—set on May 31, 1986.

PLAYING CARDS

The first paper playing cards were used in China about 2,000 years ago. Other cards used around the world were made of thin wood or ivory. The deck of cards we use today is based on a set the Chinese used both for games and as paper money.

The earliest deck is known as the Tarot cards. There were four suits of fourteen cards each. The suits stood for the class system at that time. Originally they were:

Swords—the nobility
Batons—the peasant class
Cups—the clergy (ministers and priests)
Coins—the merchant class

In the fifteenth century, the French changed the cards. The swords became spades, the batons became clubs, the cups became hearts, and the coins became diamonds.

How Many Ways?

The fifty-two cards in a deck can be rearranged 80,660,000,000, 000, 000, 000, 000, 000, 000, 000, 000, 000, 000, 000, 000, 000, 000,000, 000, 000, 000, 000 different ways.

House of Cards

In 1983, a fifteen-year-old boy, John Sain, built the largest house of cards. He used 15,714 cards from 300 decks to build sixty-eight stories for a house that was 12 feet tall and 10 inches wide.

DICE

One of the oldest games in the world is dice. Archeologists have dug into ancient ruins and found dice that were made out of peach pits, seeds, horns, pebbles, pottery, shells, beaver and woodchuck teeth, and bones from buffalo, caribou, and moose.

Perfect dice today are made by hand from plastic. They are

cubes that are perfect within ⅕,₀₀₀ of an inch. Cheaper machine-made dice aren't always perfect. Spots are drilled to a depth of ¹⁷/₁,₀₀₀ of an inch in perfect dice, and painted with paint that is the exact weight of the plastic that was drilled out. Spots are marked from one to six. Spots on opposite sides of the dice must total seven: 1 opposite 6; 2 opposite 5; 3 opposite 4.

Each one of a pair of dice—called a *die*—used in the gambling casinos is .750 of an inch square, and usually marked with the casino monogram or serial number to prevent a gambler from using his own dice.

DOMINOS

No one knows where dominos came from. They are mentioned in some Chinese texts from 1120 A.D. They may have come from dice because the spots, or pips as they are called, are arranged the same way. There are about two hundred ways to play dominos.

- *Domino stacking*: The record is 291 dominos stacked one on top of another, by David Coburn in Miami, Florida, in 1988.
- *Domino toppling*: The record is 281,581 dominos, toppled by Klaus Friedrich in 1984. It took him thirty-one days to set up the domino tiles in a line, and only twelve minutes 57.3 seconds for them all to fall down.

CHESS

There are some 318,979,564,000 possible ways to play the first four moves on each side in a game of chess. Chess came from a war game called Chaturanga played in sixth-century India. In Japan, chess is called Shogi, and in China it is called Xiang-qi.

GAME MARATHONS

Scrabble: Peter Finan and Neil Smith played 153 hours in Merseyside, England in 1985. Scrabble was invented in 1931 by Alfred M. Butts, but it wasn't trademarked as Scrabble until 1948, when James Brunot did it.

Dominos: Neil Thomas and Tim Beesley played dominos for 150 hours 5 minutes in Merseyside, England, in 1985.

Monopoly: Four players stayed at the game for 660 hours in 1981 in Atlanta, Georgia, from July 12 to August 8, 1981.

The game was invented by Charles Darrow, in Germantown, Pennsylvania, in 1933, and since then has sold more than 100 million copies in twenty-three languages.

Backgammon: Mathew Denton and Peter Royle played for 159 hours 45 minutes at St. Anselm's College, England, from August 15 to 22, 1988.

Checkers: Tom Relph and Edward Roper played checkers for 170 hours and 2 minutes at St. Anselm's College, England, from August 15 to 22, 1988.

Chess: Roger Long and Graham Croft played 200 hours of chess in Bristol, England, from May 11 to 19, 1984.

THE TEN MOST-LANDED-ON SPACES IN MONOPOLY

1. Illinois Avenue
2. Go
3. B&O Railroad
4. Free Parking
5. Tennessee Avenue
6. New York Avenue
7. Reading Railroad
8. St. James Place
9. Water Works
10. Pennsylvania Railroad

Money

CHAPTER SIX

Numbers

MONEY: WHAT IS IT?

Money is anything accepted within a country in exchange for goods or services. "Goods" are objects such as food, clothing, toys, houses, cars, or toothpicks. A "service" is something someone does for you. We pay for the services of a doctor, dentist, actor, teacher, firefighter, librarian, or life guard, for example.

Currency is the object used as money in exchanges. In this country our currency is made up of paper bills and coins—pennies, nickels, dimes, quarters, half dollars, and silver dollars. Almost anything you can imagine—and some things you can't—has been used as currency since people invented the idea of money. People used whatever was most valuable as their currency. In the Fiji Islands of the South Pacific, whales' teeth were money. Red teeth were worth twenty times more than white teeth because the red teeth were harder to find. When European explorers went to Africa in the 1800s, they found different tribes using spears, the bristles from elephants' tails, or axes for cash. In cold climates, furs were exchanged as money.

How would you like to carry some of these in your pocket?

Pigs	Rats
Stones	Whales' teeth
Feathers	Fish hooks
Eggs	Bark sleeping mats
Dogs' teeth	Drums
Coconuts	Cowrie shells
Boars' tusks	Tea
Cattle	Reindeer
Sheep	Grain
Straw	Camels
Salt	Goats
Iron	Beeswax
Bronze disks	Gold dust
Tin ingots (bars)	Lead
Oxen	Beads
Gin	Corn
Furs	Blankets
Wampum	Snails
Cacao beans	Coca leaves
Tortoise shell	Tobacco
Betel nuts	Paper
Silver	Wooden disks

Copper Rods: In the Palaboroas community in South Africa in ancient times, one copper rod bought two cows. For five copper rods a man could buy a wife.

Heavy Money

The world's heaviest money was a stone disk with a hole in the center. It was called the *fe*, and it was used on the Pacific Island of Yap until World War II. A fe could be anywhere from a few inches to 12 feet across. If one of the big stone wheels had to be moved, a pole was put through the hole so it could be carried by two strong men. Even today on Yap, people put large round stones in front of their houses to show how rich they are.

Light Money

The world's lightest money was made from feathers. These feather funds were used in the New Hebrides, which are islands in the South Pacific Ocean about 1,000 miles from Australia.

WAMPUM

The Native Americans of the northeast used strings of shells called *wampum* for currency. Wampum meant "string of white shell beads." It was convenient money because it was easy to divide, and not too bulky to carry around. But it wasn't easy to make. The Indians had only primitive tools for cutting and drilling holes in the shells. The white beads came from periwinkle shells, and the purple and black beads from the inner part of clam shells. Purple beads were more valuable than the white because they were harder to find. A belt of wampum consisted of 360 beads. The European settlers used wampum, too, because there was a shortage of European coins. In fact, wampum became legal money in Massachusetts, until some of the settlers began to make counterfeit wampum with their lathes and drills. The expression "to shell out," meaning to pay, started in the days of shell money.

ANCIENT MONEY

Egypt: In ancient Egypt, the wealthy pharoahs, or kings, didn't bother issuing money because there was so little use for it. There were only two major groups of people. The very rich people had everything that money could buy anyway, and the rest were slaves who weren't allowed to own anything. The few people who were neither slaves nor rich land owners traded for goods and services.

Greece: One of the most famous of the silver Greek coins is the **drachma**. It was worth a handful of iron nails or copper bars. One drachma could buy a sheep or an ox.

The *obol* was one-sixth of a drachma, a bit of silver no bigger than the head of a pin. People carried obols in their mouths so they wouldn't lose them. Imagine how much small change got swallowed if a person had a sudden fit of coughing!

China: In ancient China, the first money was hammered from bronze into the shapes of spades and hoes and other farming tools. Before that, the people had traded the actual tools. The metal shapes represented the most valuable things the people owned. The new currency was easier to carry around than the actual spades and hoes.

Twelve centuries before the birth of Christ (B.C.), the Chinese made coins. That was 500 years before coins were made in Europe. Among the things they had used in trade before they made coins were knives and pieces of cloth or clothing. One of the first coins, called *pu*, looked like a shirt. A coin called *tao* looked like a knife.

The first paper money was made in China in the year 1260 because the government didn't have a big enough supply of metal to make coins for 80,000,000 people. Most of the bronze and copper was being used to build statues of Buddha.

BIG AND SMALL

The largest paper money was the *kwan* note from China issued between 1368 and 1399. It was printed on sheets of mulberry-bark paper, 9 inches by 13 inches.

The smallest paper money was the 10 *bani* note made in Rumania in 1917. It was 1 inch by 1½ inches.

The biggest coin of any kind made in the world in this century is the **nugget**, produced by the Australian mint in 1991. The coin is 99.99 percent gold, with a design of a red kangaroo. It is worth $10,000, which is equal to about $7,000 in the United States. It's not likely to be carried around in anyone's pocket because the nugget is 3 inches in diameter and ½ inch thick, and it weighs 2.2 pounds (1 kilogram).

EVERYONE HAS SOMETHING TO SAY ABOUT MONEY

Penny Wise and Pound Foolish: It's an old saying to remind people that even though you may spend money carefully in small amounts, you can be wasteful when spending large amounts of money.

Money Talks: This expression started around 1900. It means that you can influence people with money. If you spend enough money, you can get anything done by paying someone to do it.

The Love of Money is the Root of All Evil: This is from the Bible, First Timothy, chapter 6, verse 10. It doesn't say that money itself is evil. It means that a person can *love* money so much that it will get him into trouble.

A Fool and His Money Are Soon Parted: This saying started in the 1500s. It is another way of saying that a foolish person spends money foolishly.

Penny Pincher: That's a very stingy person, one who won't spend money. Other words for this kind of person are *tightwad*, *miser*, and *cheapskate*.

It's Not Worth a Continental: This saying means the money's not worth anything. The first paper money made in the original Thirteen Colonies of America in 1775 was issued by the Continental Congress. Paul Revere engraved the design on the metal plates used to print the money called *"continentals."* But so many bills were printed that soon the money wasn't worth much, and people began to say of any worthless thing that "It's not worth a Continental."

Rich Man

When someone has a lot of money, people say he is *in the chips, in the bucks,* or *on Easy Street.* He has *hit the jackpot,* he's *a moneybags, loaded, well-heeled,* or he *has a pretty penny.*

Pretty Penny: In 1257 King Henry III of England issued a gold coin worth 20 shillings. When the king was forced to turn over his crown to his son, Edward, no more of the gold pieces were made. They became good luck coins then, and anyone who had one was said to have a pretty penny.

A Poor Man

When a person has no money, we say he is *poor as a churchmouse, hard up, down at the heels, flat broke, strapped, pinched, busted, stone broke, penniless, wiped out, down and out,* or that *the chips are down.*

Money Has Many Names

In slang, money has been called *cabbage, lucre, bread, long green, loot, greenback, dough, bucks, cash, moola, boodle, jack,* and *lettuce.* Can you think of any others?

What Is Pin Money?

Metal pins were invented in the 1300s, but they were expensive.
They were so scarce that in England shopkeepers were allowed
to sell pins only on January 1 and 2. At the beginning of each
year, a housewife had to ask her husband for enough "pin money"
to buy a year's supply of pins. Even after pins became plentiful
and cheap, many housewives continued to ask for their pin
money. Since then, a small allowance or gift of cash to spend as
you please has been called pin money.

Mad Money

That's the name given to extra money a young woman takes
along on a date in case she gets mad and wants to take a bus or
cab home by herself.

Where Did We Get Piggy Banks?

Craftsmen in the Middle Ages made pots and jars from a kind of
clay called *pygg*. People kept odd coins in these clay pots that

eventually became known as a pygg bank, and then, a piggy bank. Later, the banks were made to look like a pig.

WHAT IS A SALARY?

A regular paycheck earned for work is called a salary. The word comes from ancient times when salt was expensive because it was scarce. Part of the payment given to Roman soldiers was for buying salt. Some of the highways at that time were built just for transporting salt from the mines to the cities. One famous road was the Via Salarium. The salt money given to the soldiers got to be called *salarium*, and that became salary.

To "salt it away" meant that someone saved his salary. And if a person was "not worth his salt," it meant that he hadn't worked hard enough to earn it. We still use those expressions.

DON'T TAKE ANY WOODEN NICKELS

Who would take a wooden nickel? The people in the town of Tenino, Washington, did. The town's name is pronounced ten-nine-oh. It was named after its altitude, because Tenino is 1,090 feet above sea level. In 1931, the town's bank ran out of coins, so they made the first wooden nickels, which were used until the federal government sent them a supply of coins. Since then, when someone says, "Don't take any wooden nickels," they mean don't let anyone fool you.

Tally Sticks

Tenino wasn't the first place to use wooden money, however. When the Saxons from Germany invaded England in the fifth century, they made wooden coins. And they kept track of the money people owed by putting notches on sticks called "tally sticks." The stick was split, and one half was given to the person who owed the money and the other half to the person who had loaned the money. By 1834, so many thousands of these tally sticks were stored in England's House of Parliament that the government cleaned them out and burned them. Unfortunately, the fire was so huge that it got out of control and burned down Parliament!

Tellers: Bank tellers, who count out money for customers, got their name from the days of tallying. A "tallier" was the person who counted the tally sticks, and that changed over the years into teller.

WHO NAMED OUR MONEY?

Cent: In the official language of the United States government, there is no such coin as a penny. It is called the *cent*, and it got that name from a money system that was never used. In 1781 the U.S. Congress wanted to establish a system of money that would be the same for every state. Maryland and Pennsylvania and some of the other big colonies had based their money on the Spanish "piece of eight," which was worth ninety pence of English money. Merchants kept their records in "dollars and ninetieths." Robert Morris, who was superintendent of finance, suggested to Congress that the dollar should be divided into 1,440 parts. He said that a coin equal to 100 of these parts could be called a cent, from the Latin word *centum*, which meant 100. Congress didn't go for the Morris Plan, but they did choose Thomas Jefferson's suggestion to divide the dollar into 100 parts. And they did take Mr. Morris's suggestion to call that coin a cent. The penny was an English coin.

Nickel: German prospectors looking for copper in America often found rock that looked like copper, but when it was smelted or heated, it wasn't copper at all. They began to believe it really was copper, but that a gremlin or "Nicholas" or Old Nick lived in it. Their German word for it was *kupfernickel* (copper nicholas). A Swedish scientist, Axel Cronstedt, discovered that kupfernickel was a new metal. He used part of the old name and called it nickel. In 1857 an American one-cent piece was made from nickel, so it was called the nickel. The coins wore well, but they were too expensive to make. Later, the name passed to a five-cent piece made of a combination of nickel and copper, and that nickel has been used ever since.

Dime: Once the Congress had decided on the use of the dollar and the cent, it was easy to name a half dollar and a quarter dollar. But a one-tenth dollar sounded strange. So they chose the Latin word for a tenth, which is *decima*, and the coin became known as a dime. There is no silver in dimes, quarters, or half dollars. These coins are made of cuproclad, which is a combination of copper and nickel.

Dollar: In Germany, large silver coins were called "*thaler*," and that got changed into our word, dollar.

The Dollar Sign: In 1794 a coin called the "pillar dollar" was made. On it were two pillars with a ribbon twined around them. That design later became the symbol for the dollar: $.

TWO DOLLAR BILLS

The first two-dollar bills were printed in 1776, when the Continental Congress wanted to help pay for the War of Independence. The last two-dollar bills were printed in April 1976, with the portrait of Thomas Jefferson to celebrate the 200th anniversary of his birthday. It was also a way for the government to save money. We use more one-dollar bills than any other kind. But it costs just as much to print a one-dollar bill as the two, so 225,000,000 new two-dollar bills were issued, which saved about 7 million dollars. No two-dollar bills have been printed since then, but a few are still in circulation. People don't like them very much.

For some reason, two-dollar bills have been considered unlucky in this country, although they are used in other nations. Many people had the habit of tearing off a corner of a two-dollar bill before they spent it as a way of breaking any bad luck it might bring.

Three Cents' Worth: In 1851, when the government issued a three-cent stamp, they also made a three-cent coin. It didn't stay long in circulation.

FLIP A COIN

"Heads you win, tails you lose." Football games don't start until the two team captains flip a coin to see which team kicks off. Many things are decided by the flip of a coin. It started in the days of Julius Caesar. He was the first emperor to have his picture on one side of every coin made in his country. When there was an argument, the people flipped a coin. If the side showing Caesar's head landed upright, it meant the decision was final. Some coins had an animal on the side opposite the head, so that side was called "tails."

Don't Bet on It

How many times do you think you could depend on a coin's landing heads up? For a coin to fall heads up fifty times in a row, a million people would have to toss coins ten times a minute, for forty hours a week, and even then a coin would land heads up fifty times in a row only once in 900 years!

HOW LONG WOULD IT TAKE TO SPEND A BILLION DOLLARS?

If you spent one dollar each minute, it would take you about 2,000 years to spend a billion dollars.

If you lined up one billion one-dollar bills end to end, they would go around the world four times. It would take you 134 years to collect a billion dollars if you traveled around the world, working forty hours a week, and picked up one dollar bill each second.

WHY SAVE A PENNY?

If you saved one penny and doubled that amount each day (saving two cents on day two, four cents on day three, eight cents on day four, sixteen cents on day five, and so on), on the thirtieth day you would have $5,368,709.12. Really!

Penny Thief

A penny may not seem like much, but a computer expert in a bank got rich by stealing one penny at a time. His job was to keep track of the money people kept in their savings accounts. He found that he could change the computer's instructions just enough to tell it to subtract one cent from every savings account in the bank once a month. For example, if a customer had $100 in his savings, the bank paid him 46 cents at the end of the month in interest, just for letting the bank use the money. With the new instructions, the computer gave the customer only 45 cents instead of 46. Nobody noticed a penny difference. No one missed one cent. But those pennies added up quickly, and the computer expert stole millions of dollars before he was caught.

MILES OF QUARTERS

On March 16, 1985, one hundred volunteers in Atlanta, Georgia, displayed the world's longest collection of coins. There were 662,353 quarters in a line that stretched for 10 miles, 5 feet, and 7 inches. The quarters added up to $165,788.25.

WHO MAKES OUR MONEY?

The United States Department of the Treasury is in charge of all the money in this country. The Treasurer of the United States sees to it that money, stamps, and coins are made, and then destroyed when they are worn out. All the paper money is designed, engraved, and printed by the Bureau of Printing and Engraving, which is part of the United States Department of the Treasury. The Bureau also prints stamps, military certificates, and presidential invitations.

Watch Money Being Made

You can visit the Bureau of Printing and Engraving for a self-guided tour past the nine gigantic presses that turn out $40 million paper dollars a day. There are no free samples, but you can buy uncut sheets of currency in one-dollar denominations. The bureau is open to visitors Monday through Friday from 9 a.m. to 2 p.m. The address is:

14th and C Streets SW
Washington, D.C. 20228
(202) 447-0193.

The Design

After a design has been chosen for paper money, one artist engraves the portrait of the person who will appear on the bill; another artist works on the scrolls and fancy designs, and another on the lettering. The elaborate criss-cross lines filling the background of the borders are meant to make it harder for counterfeiters to copy.

Secret Ink and Paper

Paper currency is printed on sturdy paper made of cotton and linen, which is hard to tear and is made to last. Tiny red and blue silk or nylon threads scattered through the paper give it extra strength, but also make it difficult for anyone to copy. Few people know exactly what goes into the paper. Every sheet of paper is counted and well guarded at the end of each day's printing.

The ink is also made from a secret formula. Each day, ink left over from printing paper money is collected and stored by the ink-making division of the Bureau of Printing and Engraving. In a year, the Bureau uses more than 1,500 tons of ink and more than 1,100 tons of paper.

COUNTERFEITERS

These are criminals who try to make fake money that looks real enough to fool anyone. Even if very talented counterfeiters could engrave perfect copies of the metal plates used for printing money, it's unlikely that they'd also be able to match the paper and ink perfectly. But still they try!

It's even harder to copy money since the new Series 1990 one hundred dollar bill was made. Running through the new bill from top to bottom is a polyester security thread printed with "USA 100" in very tiny letters that can't be copied in a copy machine. If you hold one of these bills up to the light, you can see the thread between the border and the Federal Reserve Seal on the left. In a narrow band around Benjamin Franklin's portrait the words "The United States of America" are engraved in type that is also too small to copy. Next, the Bureau of Engraving and Printing plans to make new counterfeit-proof fifty-dollar bills and then twenties, tens, and fives.

Minting Coins

The Bureau of the Mint, which is also part of the Treasury Department, manufactures and distributes coins and medals, and stores gold and silver. The address of the Mint is:

501 13th St. NW
Washington, D.C. 20220

The phone number is (202) 376-0837. There are branches of the Mint in Philadelphia, Pennsylvania; Denver, Colorado; and San Francisco, California.

Some gold and silver is stored at West Point, New York. About 9,000 tons of gold, worth about $90 million, are kept at Fort Knox, Kentucky, in a bomb-proof building called the U.S. Bullion Repository. But the biggest hoard of gold, 14,000 tons, is kept in the Federal Reserve Bank in New York City. Some of it is safe in vaults 85 feet below the city streets. Not all the stored gold belongs to the United States. Forty other nations store gold there, too. Four men, working in two shifts, have the job of carting money from one nation's vault to another as different deals are made between countries.

Money Packs

Coins are bagged at the Mint and sent to banks in bags of: cents = $50 per bag; nickels = $200 per bag; dimes, quarters, and half dollars = $1,000 per bag.

Dollar bills are put into bundles of 100. Those bundles are put into packages of 40. Each package weighs 8½ pounds. Ones come in packages of $4,000; fives come in packages of $20,000; tens in packages of $40,000; twenties in packages of $80,000; fifties in packages of $200,000; and one-hundred-dollar bills in packages of $400,000.

WHAT'S ON OUR MONEY?

"In God We Trust": That slogan first appeared on a U.S. coin in 1864. In 1955, Congress made the slogan official on all currency.

"E Pluribus Unum": The Latin phrase on U.S. coins means "one out of many."

Who's Who on Our Coins?

All coins made today honor past presidents. There's one exception: Susan B. Anthony is on a one-dollar coin. She led the fight for women's right to vote.

Abraham Lincoln is on the penny.
Thomas Jefferson is on the nickel.
Franklin Delano Roosevelt is on the dime.
George Washington is on the quarter.
John Kennedy is on the half dollar, or fifty cent piece.
Dwight D. Eisenhower is on the silver dollar, which was last made in 1978.

Once a coin has been issued, the design cannot be changed for twenty-five years, except by an act of Congress.

Celebrations: Sometimes special coins are minted to celebrate historic events or great accomplishments or famous people. In 1987, a silver dollar was made to celebrate the 200th anniversary of the United States Constitution. In 1990, the Mint made the Eisenhower silver dollar in honor of General Dwight D. Eisenhower, who was the thirty-fourth president of the United States. In 1991, a series of gold, silver, and lead coins was made for the fiftieth anniversary of Mount Rushmore, which was finished in 1941.

For More Information About Coins, you can write to:
United States Mint
10001 Aerospace Rd.
Lanham, MD 20706

Who's on Our Paper Money?

George Washington is on the one-dollar bill.
Abraham Lincoln is on the five-dollar bill.
Alexander Hamilton is on the ten-dollar bill.
Andrew Jackson is on the twenty-dollar bill.
Ulysses S. Grant is on the fifty-dollar bill.
Thomas Jefferson is on the one-hundred-dollar bill.

You probably won't see many of the higher denomination bills from $500 to $10,000 because they are no longer printed. When they do show up at banks, the bills are taken out of circulation.

William McKinley is on the 500-dollar bill.
Grover Cleveland is on the 1,000-dollar bill.
James Madison is on the 5,000-dollar-bill.
Salmon P. Chase is on the 10,000-dollar bill.
Woodrow Wilson is on the 100,000-dollar bill, but this one
    was never put into circulation.

No Live Ones

By law, no living person's image may be on coins or bills. That law was passed after the Civil War when Spencer C. Clark was chief clerk of the National Currency Division of the U.S. Treasury (which became the Bureau of Engraving). Clark used his own picture on 500,000 five-cent notes before Congress decided that wasn't a great idea.

No Women

There are no women pictured on U.S. paper currency now in circulation. Martha Washington's portrait was on the face of the silver dollar certificate (paper money) issued in 1886 and in 1891. In 1896, she was on the reverse side of a silver certificate. Pocahontas was on the back of the twenty-dollar bill issued in 1875.

How Much Money is There?

The value of all the currency—coin and paper money—kept in circulation in the United States is $199,000,000,000.

WHERE DOES THE OLD MONEY GO?

How long does a dollar bill last? Anywhere from six to eighteen months. A five lasts about a year, and a ten-dollar bill about a year and a half. A twenty-dollar bill lasts from thirty to forty-five months. Bills are considered worn out when they flunk a test in a huge machine that can check them at the rate of 60,000 bills an hour.

If you have both halves of an old bill that's been torn in half, the bank will give you a new one. But if you have only a part of a bill, you must have at least three-quarters of it in order to exchange it for its regular value.

A TENPENNY NAIL

In the early days of America, before a nail-making machine was invented in the late 1700s, nails were scarce and valuable because they had to be made by hand. It was common to use them as money. There were ten-penny nails and two-penny nails, for example. In hardware stores today those names are still used to indicate different sized nails.

PIECES OF EIGHT AND TWO BITS

When the Spanish settled Florida, they used a gold coin called a *real*. Each real was worth about 12½ cents. A Spanish silver dollar was worth 8 reales, and pirates called the silver dollars *pesos de ocho*, which means "pieces of eight."

The slang word for real was a *bit*. When people couldn't find any small coins, or when they wanted to make change, they cut the silver dollars into four parts. Each part was worth two reales, or two bits. That's why the slang for a quarter is still "two bits" and a half dollar is "four bits."

MONEY AROUND THE WORLD

The dollar is the name of the common currency in the United States, Canada, New Zealand, the Bahamas, Singapore, and several other nations, but that doesn't mean those dollars have equal value. There is a Swiss franc, a French franc, and a franc in Central Africa, but they are all worth different amounts. A lira in Turkey is not the same as a lira in Italy.

Here are some of the different kinds of currencies used around the world:

Afghanistan	afghani
Algeria	dinar
Argentina	austral
Australia	dollar
Austria	schilling
Belgium	franc
Boliva	peso
Brazil	cruzado
Bulgaria	lev
Burma	kyat
Cambodia	riel
Chile	peso
China	yuan
Costa Rica	colon
Cuba	peso
Czechoslovakia	koruna
Denmark	krone
Dominican Republic	peso
Ecuador	sucre
Egypt	pound
El Salvador	colon
Ethiopia	birr
Fiji	dollar
Finland	markka
France	franc
Germany	mark
Greece	drachma
Guatemala	quetzal

Haiti	gourde
Honduras	lempira
Hungary	forint
Iceland	krona
India	rupee
Indonesia	rupiah
Iran	rial
Iraq	dinar
Ireland	pound
Israel	shekel
Italy	lira
Japan	yen
Jordon	dinar
Kenya	shilling
Korea (North and South)	won
Kuwait	dinar
Laos	kip
Lebanon	pound
Libya	dollar
Liechtenstein	Swiss franc
Malaysia	ringgit
Mexico	peso
Mongolia	tugrik
Morocco	dirham
Nepal	rupee
Netherlands	guilder
New Zealand	dollar
Nicaragua	cordoba
Nigeria	naira
Norway	krone
Panama	balboa
Paraguay	guarani
Peru	inti

Philippines	peso
Poland	zloty
Portugal	escudo
Rumania	lei
Russia	ruble
Saudi Arabia	riyal
Singapore	dollar
South Africa	rand
Spain	peseta
Sudan	pound
Sweden	krona
Switzerland	franc
Taiwan	New Taiwan dollar
Turkey	lira
United Arab Emirates	dirham
United Kingdom	pound sterling
United States	dollar
Uruguay	peso
Vatican City	lira
Venezuela	bolivar
Vietnam	dong
Yemen	dinar
Yugoslavia	dinar
Zaire	zaire
Zambia	kwacha

BANKS

The first banks were in Venice, Italy, during the Middle Ages. The bankers sat on benches in the open marketplaces. The benches were called *bancos* in Italian, which gave us our word "bank."

I.O.U.: These initials mean "I owe you" money. If you borrow money from someone, you can write an I.O.U. note, which is your promise to pay them back.

Checks: A check is a kind of I.O.U. Instead of carrying money, a person uses a paper note that tells a bank to pay that person the amount written on the check. You have to have money in the bank, of course. It works like this: If you bought an old bicycle from Bill Smith for $30, but you didn't have the money with you, you could write a check to Bill Smith. Mr. Smith would take your check to the bank, and they would pay him the $30. If you had only $20 in your bank account, your check would "*bounce*." In other words, the teller would hand the check back to Bill Smith and say, "Sorry, but we can't cash this. There isn't enough money in the account." The expression "*rubber check*" means that a check wasn't any good, that it bounced back.

Credit Cards: With "plastic money" we can "buy now and pay later." You hand a plastic credit card to a clerk in a store to buy shoes, for example. The company that handles the credit cards pays the store for the shoes. But then they send you a bill, and you must pay the credit card company. If you don't pay on time, it will cost you extra. The newest credit cards are called "*smart cards*" because they have embedded in them a tiny microchip that can hold instant information about the card's owner—not only the name, address, and bank code number, but how much money is in his bank account, and what bills he hasn't paid.

ATM: An Automatic Teller Machine does the work of a human teller. A person who wants to withdraw money puts a plastic card into the machine; the machine's computer reads that person's code, checks that person's bank balance, and triggers the mechanism that counts out the money. Money can also be deposited in an ATM.

WHO INVENTED BUDGETS?

When your parents tell you to "budget" your allowance, it's not something they thought up. The idea started in ancient Rome, when women paid the family bills and managed the money. If a wife had to pay for five different things, she divided the money into five small leather bags, labeled for food, cloth, grain, or whatever she had to buy. In the Latin language spoken in Rome, the bag was called a *bulga*. Later, the French people borrowed the idea of dividing up the money, only they called the bags *bougette*. The English people learned from the French, and gradually this way of doling out money carefully was called a budget.

ARE YOU A NUMISMATIST
(New-Miss-Mat-Ist)?

If you are, you have lots of company. A numismatist is a coin collector. Millions of people enjoy this hobby. You can get information from:

American Numismatic Society
155th and Broadway
New York, NY 10032

The American Numismatic Association also has a library and a coin museum, and it publishes a newsletter called *The Numismatist*. The address is:

American Numismatic Association
P.O. Box 2366
Colorado Springs, CO 80903

Another museum of coins, stamps, and paper money, and source of information is:

Boys Town PhilMatic Center
13628 Father Flanagan Blvd.
Boys Town, NE 68010

Worth Its Weight in Gold

The highest price ever paid at an auction for a single coin was $725,000, in 1979, for a gold coin called the Brasher Doubloon made in 1787. There are only six of these coins in the world.

It Looks Fine

Old coins are graded by their appearance. The better the coin looks, the more it is worth. This is how collectors judge coins:

Fair: so worn that it can just about be identified
Good: very worn, but outline of design visible
Very good: design shows clearly but detail is worn away
Fine: shows signs of wear
Very fine: shows slight wear
Extra fine: almost perfect
Uncirculated: in mint condition, like new

Proof Coin: Proof coins are made just for collections. They are not to be spent. Each coin has a perfect mirror-like shine.

Guide Books

Two books coin collectors use to find the value of their coins are:

Official Black Book
Price Guide of United States Coins, by Marc Hudgeons
The House of Collectibles
Ballantine Books
New York, New York

A Guide Book of United States Coins
The Official Red Book of U.S. Coins, by R. S. Yeoman
Western Publishing Co.
Racine, Wisconsin

People

CHAPTER SEVEN

Numbers

BLOOD AND GUTS

- If all of your blood vessels were attached end to end, they would make a tube more than 60,000 miles long. When you are grown, you'll have 100,000 miles of blood vessels, enough to go around the equator about four times.
- The human heart beats about 72 times a minute. That's 104,000 times a day; 38 million times each year. By the time you are sixty years old, your heart will have beaten more than 2,000,300,000 times.
- Each person has about 1 quart of blood for every 25 pounds he weighs. So a person who weighs 100 pounds has about 4 quarts of blood. All of your blood circulates through your body 1,000 times each day.
- We have about 5 million red blood cells in each drop of blood, or about 25 trillion red blood cells in our entire body.
- The human heart pumps 10,500 quarts of blood through the blood vessels in a day, and 264 million quarts of blood in a lifetime. That's enough blood to fill 6,600 tank cars. That many tank cars lined up would be 50 miles long.

- In one day, a human heart does enough work to lift a 65-ton tank car 2 feet off the ground. If you are thirteen years old now, your heart has already done enough work to lift a battleship 2½ feet.

HAIRY NUMBERS

- We have anywhere from 100,000 to 150,000 hairs on our heads. Hair grows about ½ inch each month. Each hair lasts three to five years. It's normal to lose 50 to 100 hairs each day.
- It takes about eight weeks for a man's beard to grow an inch. Someone at the Gillette Safety Razor Company figured out that a man could save himself 3,350 hours if he never shaved. But by the time he was an old man, the nonshaver would be dragging around a beard 30 feet long, and every sixteen years his beard would weigh another pound.
- Apparently no one has ever gone that long without shaving because the longest beard on record, measured in 1912, was 11 feet, 6 inches long.

NAIL NUMBERS

- Did you know that your fingernails grow more slowly in winter than in summer? But they grow faster than toenails.
- It takes about three months for a whole fingernail to replace itself. The nails on your thumb and middle finger grow faster than the others.
- Forty percent of all children and teenagers bite their nails. But it's a losing battle because the more they bite, the faster the nails grow in again.

MUSCLE NUMBERS

- A human has about 639 muscles. In saying one word, we use 72 muscles.

- A smile uses less energy than a frown. It takes 17 muscles to smile, but 43 to frown.

SKIN NUMBERS

- Skin is the body's largest organ. The average person is covered by 14 to 18 square feet of skin, and that weighs about 6 pounds.
- We shed our skin in tiny bits and pieces, enough to replace the top layer of dead cells every twenty-seven days. In a lifetime, you will have more than 1,000 new layers of skin. Thousands of cells wash away each time you wash your hands!
- We have between 2 to 5 million sweat glands in our skin, especially on the palms of our hands and the soles of our feet. In an hour of hard exercise on a hot day, an adult can lose 54 ounces of body fluid in sweat.

THE NOSE KNOWS

- The human nose can recognize about 1,000 different smells.
- In one day, more than 2,500 gallons of air flow through the nose.

BRAINY NUMBERS

- When you are born, your brain weighs about 12 ounces, and by the time you are grown up, your brain will weigh about 3 pounds.
- The brain grows fastest during the first three years of life. By the time you are six, your brain is about 90 percent as big as it will ever be. But the size of the brain means nothing— Einstein's brain was only average size.
- We are born with all the nerve cells the brain will ever have— about 100 billion. About ten billion of them are neurons.

These are the electrochemical switches that send and receive messages. It is these neurons that grow. As we learn, the number and size of connections between neurons increases. Brain cells die every day. Brain cells damaged by drugs, alcohol, aging, disease, or accident are never replaced.

NOT MADE OF SUGAR AND SPICE

The old rhyme says "Sugar and spice and everything nice, that's what little girls are made of." And "Snips and snails and puppy dog tails, that's what little boys are made of." Not likely! We're all made of water, iron, carbon, and dozens of other elements.

- If all the iron in a human body could be collected, there would be enough to make a 3-inch nail. But if all the carbon could be collected, there'd be enough to make 900 pencils.
- Two-thirds of the human body is water. Even your brain is 74 percent water!
- In a lifetime, a person will drink about 16,000 gallons of water.
- In a year, an average American eats 1,417 pounds of food.

LONGEST YAWN, HICCUP, AND SNEEZE

- The longest attack of hiccups lasted 65 years.
- The longest sneezing session lasted 978 days.
- The longest yawning lasted 5 weeks.
- A cough explodes from the mouth at 60 miles an hour!

BONE COUNT

- *The largest bone* in the human body is the *femur*, the long leg bone that connects the hip to the knee.

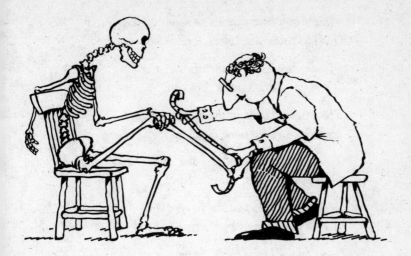

- *The smallest bone* is the *stirrup* in the ear. Its scientific name is stapes. It is one of three tiny bones—the hammer, anvil, and stirrup—that allow us to hear.
- There are 206 bones in the human body. This old rhyme helps people remember how many bones in each part of the body:

> *How many bones in the human face?*
> *Fourteen, when they're all in place.*
>
> *How many bones in the human head?*
> *Eight, my child, as I've often said.*
>
> *How many bones in the human ear?*
> *Three in each, and they help to hear.*
>
> *How many bones in the human spine?*
> *Twenty-six, like a climbing vine.*
>
> *How many bones in the human chest?*
> *Twenty-four ribs and two of the rest.*

How many bones in the shoulder bind?
Two in each, one before, one behind.

How many bones in the arms of man?
Three in each; count if you can.

How many bones in the human wrist?
Eight in each, if none is missed.

How many bones in the palm of the hand?
Five in each, with many a band.

How many bones in the fingers ten?
Twenty-eight, and by joints they bend.

How many bones in the human hip?
One in each, like a dish they dip.

How many bones in the human thigh?
One in each, and deep they lie.

How many bones in the human knees?
One in each, the kneecap, please.

How many bones from foot to knee?
Two in each, we plainly see.

How many bones in the ankle strong?
Seven in each, but none is long.

How many bones in the ball of the foot?
Five in each, as the palms were put.

How many bones in the toes, half a score?
Twenty-eight, and there are no more.

And now altogether these many bones fix,
And they count in the body two hundred and six.

EYE FACTS

Do you wear glasses? If you do, you have lots of company. Forty-six percent—almost half—of the people in the United States wear glasses or contact lenses.

What Is 20/20 Vision?

20/20 is normal distance vision, measured in feet. You look at an eye chart placed 20 feet away. If you can read lines that normal eyes can see at 20 feet, you have 20/20 vision. If you can read only the lines that normal eyes can read at a distance of 40 feet, you have 20/40 vision. Your two eyes can be different. One eye might be 20/20 and the other 20/40. A person who sees distant things better than things close is said to be **far-sighted**.

A person with better close vision is said to be **near-sighted**. Close vision is measured as 14/14. For example, if your eye is 14/50, it means that you have to be within 14 inches to read letters that normal eyes can see 50 inches away. If you are near-sighted, you may need to sit at the front of the classroom to read the blackboard.

BODY TEMPERATURE

98.6 degrees Fahrenheit is an average normal body temperature. But "normal" is different for different people. A normal temperature for one person might be 99 degrees, and for another it could be 98.2 or 97. If the body's temperature gets too high or too low, the person cannot live. The brain is damaged if the body temperature reaches 108 degrees F, and a person will become unconscious if his body temperature drops to 91 degrees F.

WHAT DOES BLOOD PRESSURE MEAN?

Blood pressure is the force of blood going through the arteries. It's a lot like the force of water going through a hose, which can be at high pressure or low. A healthy blood pressure is 120/80, or 120/70. The first number is the pressure of the blood when the heart muscle contracts and pumps blood through the arteries. The second number is the pressure of the blood when the heart relaxes between beats.

CELL FACTS

There are 50 trillion cells in the human body. Billions of them die and are replaced every day.

- Red blood cells last about 120 days.
- White blood cells called lymphocytes last a year.
- Other white blood cells live about 10 hours.
- Platelets, which allow blood to clot, are replaced after 10 days.
- Stomach cells are replaced every 2 days.
- Skin cells last anywhere from 19 to 34 days.
- Brain cells are never replaced.

HOW FAST DOES PAIN TRAVEL?

If you burn your fingertip, that message races to your brain in one-fiftieth of a second. Fast pain travels by express, no stops on its way to the brain. Slow pain, such as throbbing or aching, may make stops, starts, and detours through different nerve endings.

MY, HOW YOU'VE GROWN!

People are getting taller! The average man today would not fit into a suit of armor worn by knights in the Middle Ages. The knights may have been the best athletes of their day, well fed, and healthier than the peasants, but they were short by today's standards. Houses built 300 or 400 years ago had lower ceilings than our houses today, which means the people must have been shorter or they would have bumped their heads.

Has anyone ever said to you, "My, how you've grown! *You must have grown overnight.*" Well, actually you have. Children do grow at night. There are four stages of sleep. Stage one, as you drift off to sleep, lasts five or six minutes. Then you move into stage two, but if someone wakes you, you'll insist you haven't been sleeping. When you are in the third stage, sound asleep, your heart rate slows, and your temperature and blood pressure drop just a bit. That's when the brain releases a growth hormone, and you really grow overnight. Stage four is when you dream.

PEOPLE COUNT

Not long after George Washington became the first president of the United States, the first **census** took place, as required by Article I, Section II, of the U.S. Constitution. A census is a count of the population.

In 1790, there were 3,929,326 people in the new nation by actual count. Thomas Jefferson, who was in charge of the census, thought the real number was probably closer to 4,100,000. U.S. marshals had counted all the free white males age sixteen and over, and those under sixteen, in order to find out how many men might be available for military service. They also counted all free white females, and other free persons, which included Indians who paid taxes. Slaves were counted separately.

Why Do We Need a Census?

Every country counts its citizens to find out how many people live there. They also need to know how many children have been born so they can plan to have enough schools. And it's important to see which sections of the country are growing in order to plan for gas, electricity, water, housing, and transportation.

But the most important reason for a census in America is to decide how many people a state will have represented in Congress. In the United States, we, the people, are represented by two senators from each state. But the number of congressmen each state sends to the House of Representatives in Washington, D.C., depends upon how many people live in that state. New Jersey is much smaller in size than Alaska, but New Jersey has many more people, so it has fourteen congressmen while Alaska has only one.

We're Growing!

Since that first one, a census has been taken every ten years for the past 200 years. It always starts on April first of any year ending in zero. A baby born on April 2, 1990, for example, will not be counted until the census of April 1, 2000.

In 1990, there were 250 million people in the United States. The nation is growing at the rate of 6,300 people each day. Every 8 seconds a baby is born. Every 14 seconds someone dies. One immigrant arrives in America from another country every 35 seconds, and 1 person leaves every 3 minutes. At that rate, there will be 300 million people living in the United States by the year 2020.

To count all those people in the 1990 census, more than 500,000 people were needed to work at 484 offices around the country. It cost more than $2.5 billion to take the census, organize the information, and send out the results.

Signs,

CHAPTER EIGHT

Symbols, Scales, and Codes

If you were stranded on a boat in the middle of the ocean, how would you signal for help? How would you read if you were blind? What's a niner, a big ten-four, or double eighty-eights in CB language? What does a skull and crossbones mean? What's a bar code? Who is Mohs, and what does his scale measure? If you want to know how to sign your name in sign language or make up a code of your own, this is the chapter for you.

THE MORSE CODE

Samuel F. B. Morse tapped out the world's first telegraph message from the Capitol Building in Washington, D.C., to Baltimore, Maryland in May 1844. It said, "What hath God wrought!" Actually, it was Morse's associate, Alfred L. Vail, who worked out the details of the dots and dashes for the Morse Code. In 1851, the code became the International Morse Code or the Continental Code. It was a very handy code to learn because it could be sent over a wire as dots and dashes, or tapped on a wall, or flashed by light, or written on paper. The letter *e* is used most often in the English language, so Morse gave it the shortest code, a single dot. The letters *j*, *q*, and *y* are least used, so he assigned them the longest codes.

A:	Alpha ·—	P:	Papa ·——·		4:	····—
B:	Bravo —···	Q:	Quebec (kaybec) ——·—		5:	·····
C:	Charlie —·—·	R:	Romeo ·—·		6:	—····
D:	Delta —··	S:	Sierra ···		7:	——···
E:	Echo ·	T:	Tango —		8:	———··
F:	Foxtrot ··—·	U:	Uniform ··—		9:	————·
G:	Golf ——·	V:	Victor ···—		10:	—————
H:	Hotel ····	W:	Whiskey ·——	period:	·—·—·—
I:	India ··	X:	X-ray —··—	comma:	——··——
J:	Juliet ·———	Y:	Yankee —·——	question mark:	··——··
K:	Kilo —·—	Z:	Zulu ——··	semicolon:	—·—·—·
L:	Lima (leema) ·—··	1:	·————	colon:	———···
M:	Mike ——	2:	··———	hyphen:	—····—
N:	November —·	3:	···——	apostrophe:	·————·
O:	Oscar ———				

SOS

The most famous code is the call for help, SOS. Dit dit dit. Dah dah dah. Dit dit, dit. Three dots, three dashes, and three dots; or three short flashes of light, three long, and three short. Morse used SOS because the three dots and three dashes for *s* and *o* were easy to remember. The letters had no special meaning. It wasn't until 1912 that SOS became the official international distress signal. One of the first ships to send the SOS was the British liner *Titanic*, after it struck an iceberg and sank on its first voyage across the Atlantic Ocean. After that, people were sure the SOS meant Save Our Souls, or Save Our Ship.

The SOS signal is now sent by computer, by way of a satellite orbiting the earth. No longer is the signal made up of dots and dashes. On the computer the code now is: 1010011 1001111 1010011.

SEMAPHORE CODE

A semaphore code is signaled with flags or lights. Before the invention of the telegraph, semaphore signals were sent from high towers. Boy scouts and sailors still learn semaphore. If enemy submarines are nearby, a ship can keep its radios silent and still send silent semaphores to other ships in its fleet. Railroads send semaphore by moveable mechanical arms and rows of lights on high towers to let trains know when tracks have been switched.

INTERNATIONAL DISTRESS FLAGS

Flags have been used to send messages from ships since the time of the Roman Empire. In the 1300s, the British used flags to signal when the enemy was in sight, and by raising and lowering the flags, they could also tell how many ships the enemy had.

Today, ships use the International Code, with twenty-six flags to represent the twenty-six letters of the alphabet; one code flag; one answering flag; three repeater flags to tell you to repeat the

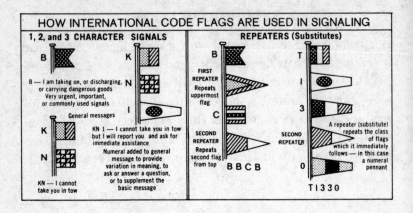

HOW INTERNATIONAL CODE FLAGS ARE USED IN SIGNALING

last flag; and ten numeral flags. Messages are made up of groups of flags.

If you were stranded in the ocean and your engines had died, you would hoist up the code flag first. Next you'd hoist the L and the O because *LO* means, "My engines are disabled." Anyone seeing that code would get your message even if they didn't speak English. And they would hoist an answer pennant to tell you they saw your message, and probably send a message of their own. If you had hoisted only the O flag, they would have read it as "Man overboard." *NC* would mean you needed immediate help.

MAYDAY, MAYDAY

The International Convention for the Safety of Life at Sea says that a ship's captain who sees or hears any of the following distress calls or signals is legally obliged to help. The call "Mayday, mayday" over the ship's radio is used only when the ship is in grave danger and needs immediate help. The word comes from the French *m'aidez*, which means "help me."

The other official signals for help are:

INTERNATIONAL FLAGS AND PENNANTS

ALPHABET FLAGS			NUMERAL PENNANTS
Alfa — Diver Down; Keep Clear	**Kilo** — Desire to Communicate	**Uniform** — Standing into Danger	**1**
Bravo — Dangerous Cargo	**Lima** — Stop Instantly	**Victor** — Require Assistance	**2**
Charlie — Yes	**Mike** — I Am Stopped	**Whis-key** — Require Medical Assistance	**3**
Delta — Keep Clear	**November** — No	**X ray** — Stop Your Intention	**4**
Echo — Altering Course to Starboard	**Oscar** — Man Overboard	**Yankee** — Am Dragging Anchor	**5**
Foxtrot — Disabled	**Papa** — About to Sail	**Zulu** — Require a Tug	**6**
Golf — Want a Pilot	**Quebec** — Request Pratique	REPEATERS — **1st Repeat**	**7**
Hotel — Pilot on Board	**Romeo**	**2nd Repeat**	**8**
India — Altering Course to Port	**Sierra** — Engines Going Astern	**3rd Repeat**	**9**
Juliett — On Fire; Keep Clear	**Tango** — Keep Clear of Me	**CODE** and Answering Pennant (Decimal Point)	**0**

WHITE   BLUE   RED   YELLOW   BLACK

- Gun or explosive fired at 1-minute intervals
- Continuous sounding of fog signal, such as a foghorn
- Rockets throwing red stars fired at one-minute intervals
- Morse Code SOS (three dots, three dashes, three dots), sent by any means available
- International Code flag NC (with flag N above flag C)
- A square flag with anything above or below it resembling a ball
- Flames on a vessel, such as oily rags or burning tar
- Red parachute flare or red hand flare
- Orange smoke
- The slow raising and lowering of outstretched arms.

CB TALK

Truckers on the road talk to each other through Citizen Band radios. Here are some of the words and numbers they use in the CB code:

Big 10-4 = okay
Big 8s = sign off, best wishes
Double 88s = love and kisses
Double 7 = no, or no contact
5 by 9 = he's getting a clear, strong radio contact
4-2 = perhaps or maybe
4-roger = yes
4-wheeler = a car
4-wheeler fever = a car in trouble
Gimmie 5 = speak to me for a few minutes
Go 10-100 = he's stopping to go to the bathroom
Meeting 20 = a meeting place
Niner = an emergency
Ten bye-bye = good-bye

PHONETIC MESSAGES

Phonetic messages are used frequently in military communications. It's a way of sounding out the letters of the alphabet so the person hearing the message doesn't make any mistakes. For example, to spell out the name of a meeting place, the caller might say, "Kuwait—kilo, uniform, whiskey, alpha, India, tango." Or "This is Charlie-unit," when he means C Unit.
N = November

A = alpha	N = November
B = bravo	O = Oscar
C = Charlie	P = papa
D = delta	Q = Quebec
E = echo	R = Romeo
F = foxtrot	S = Sierra
G = golf	T = tango
H = hotel	U = uniform
I = India	V = victor
J = Juliet	W = whiskey
K = kilo	X = x-ray
L = lima	Y = yankee
M = Mike	Z = Zulu

BRAILLE

Braille is a code used by blind people made up of sixty-three characters formed by patterns of six raised dots. It is read by running your fingers over the dots. Louis Braille invented the code in 1824, when he was only fifteen years old. He had been blind since he was three. He patterned his system after the "night writing" that was used by the French army for nighttime battlefield communication. Special editions of books and magazines are written in Braille so that blind people can read. Four dots in

a	b	c	d	e	f	g	h	i	j
1	2	3	4	5	6	7	8	9	0

k	l	m	n	o	p	q	r	s	t

u	v	w	x	y	z	Capital Sign	Numeral Sign

the shape of a backward L placed in front of the first ten letters of the alphabet turn that letter into a number.

BANK CODES

When your parents go to the money machine at the bank, they have to put a plastic card into the slot. But before the machine accepts the card, it has to "read" the code your parents have chosen. Sometimes people use their house number, or their initials, or their birthdate, or a pet's name. Experts say it's better to use a code not so easy to guess. They tell card owners to use mixed-up letters or nonsense words nobody else would know. If your school uses plastic cards to open lockers, make sure your code is so weird that even your best friend would never guess what combination of letters or numbers you chose.

SIGNING

Signing is a sign language used by deaf people. In one system, a person spells out words, using fingers to shape the letters. In the Amslan sign language, whole words or phrases are represented by hand signs. Most people use a combination of these systems.

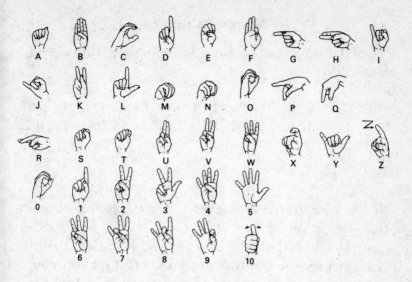

OLD CODE

On April 18, 1775, before Paul Revere rode his horse from Boston into the countryside to warn people that the British troops were coming, he looked for a coded message hanging in the steeple of North Church. He and his friends had agreed that the message would be, "One if by land, two if by sea." If the British army was marching overland, one lantern would hang in the steeple. If the British were arriving by ship, two lanterns would shine from the church tower.

CIPHERS

A code is a system of letters, signals, or symbols with special meanings, used to send messages. A cipher is the specific set of numbers, letters, or symbols used to make up the whole code. You don't have to be a spy to use a coded message. Make a code of your own. It could come in handy if you don't want everyone to read your message.

Number Cipher

One of the easiest codes uses numbers in place of letters of the alphabet, like this:

A B C D E F G H I J K L M N O P Q R S T
1 2 3 4 5 6 7 8 9 10 11 12 13 14 15 16 17 18 19 20

U V W X Y Z
21 22 23 24 25 26

If you want to send the message: *Meet me after school*, you would write it like this:

13-5-5-20   13-5   1-6-20-5-18   19-3-8-15-15-12

But that's such an easy code to figure out that you may want to make it more difficult. You can turn it around and use the alphabet backwards so that 1 = Z and 26 = A. Whatever cipher you use, make sure the friend who will receive your message knows how to decode it.

Number Shift Cipher

To make the code just a bit more difficult, you can shift the numbers. Write the alphabet across the page. Choose a key number and place that number above the A. Then finish numbering the alphabet from that number. Make sure your partner knows the key number.

If your key is number 9, this is what your cipher will look like:

9 10 11 12 13 14 15 16 17 18 19 20 21 22 23 24 25 26 27
A B C D E F G H I J K L M N O P Q R S

28 29 30 31 32 33 34
T U V W X Y Z

Can you read this message, using the key number of 9?

9-22-22   20-17-19-13-27   33-23-29

Tic Tac Toe Cipher

Here's another one. In this cipher, the symbols will be easy to figure out once you see how it's made. Draw a large tic tac toe board. Put three letters in alphabetical order, one below the other, into each space. Because the last level has only y and z, you can add a question mark there if you want to. It will look like this:

This is what the symbols will look like:

The message *Meet me at one* will look like this:

Can you read this message?

┌◻∟ ⅃⌐⅂⅃ ⅂ㄴ - ⅂⊓◻⅃ㄴ

A CODE WITHOUT SYMBOLS

You can send invisible messages if you don't want anyone to see it. You don't need fancy invisible ink if you have a little vinegar, lemon juice, orange juice, Coca Cola, Dr. Pepper, or Pepsi in the house. You can also use onion juice, but one whiff of your note and someone's sure to know that you either have a secret message or onions in your lunch.

Do *not* use an old, empty ballpoint pen to write your invisible message because that leaves marks on the paper that are too easy to read. The best tool is a Popsicle stick or a wooden matchstick. Dip the stick in the liquid and write your message. When it dries, you can't see it.

To read it, your partner should hold the paper over a light bulb. The heat from the bulb will soon turn the dried vinegar or juice brown. Do *not* heat it over a candle or a stove or a match. If it catches fire, you won't have a message at all.

ZIP CODES

Millions and millions of letters are mailed every day. How do they get to each address so accurately? In 1963, the U.S. Postal Service started the Zoning Improvement Plan, called ZIP, to use with computer sorting. Every post office was given a five-digit number code. The numbers that start with zeros are farthest east. The zip code for Adjuntas, Puerto Rico, is 00601. Places farthest west start with nines. The zip for Ketchikan, Alaska, is 99950. This is what the five numbers mean:

ZIP CODE NATIONAL AREAS

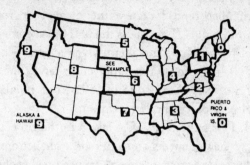

The first digit of a ZIP Code divides the country into 10 large groups of states numbered from 0 in the Northeast to 9 in the far west.

EXAMPLE

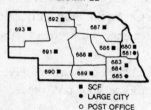

Within these areas, each state is divided into an average of 10 smaller geographic areas, identified by the 2nd and 3rd digits of the ZIP Code.

WHAT YOUR ZIP CODE MEANS

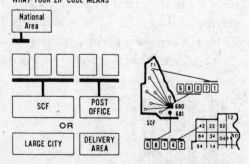

The 4th and 5th digits identify a local delivery area.

Source: U.S. Postal Service 1988 National Five-Digit ZIP Code and Post Office Directory. Used with permission.

The zip code for a town near Buffalo, New York, is 14032. The first number stands for one of the ten areas or groups of states in the United States. The 1 tells the post office computer to send the letter to the New York-Pennsylvania area. The next two numbers, 40, tell the postal employee to send that letter on to one section of New York state. The last two numbers, 32, tell what local post office the letter goes to.

In 1983, four more digits were added to the zip code. The first of these two new numbers are codes for a smaller area, such as a few city blocks, or a group of streets, or even one big office building. The last two numbers pinpoint a post office box, a single floor of a building, or a department in a large company or factory.

All the senators have their Washington, D.C., offices in the Senate Office Building with a zip code of 20510. All congressmen work in the House of Representatives Office Building with a zip code of 20515. All government departments and agencies have their own zip code.

You can get a copy of the U.S. Postal Service National Five-Digit ZIP Code and Post Office Directory at your post office.

BAR CODES

Almost everything we buy today is marked by a bar code. It's also called a UPC or universal product code. They were first used in grocery stores in 1973 for the computer check-outs that were being developed then. A laser light "reads" the light and dark,

0 70989 39641 8

thick and thin black bars. Wide bars take longer to read than thin ones. This difference in time is changed into digits by the computer. The code does not include the price of the item because prices change often, and two stores might have different prices for the same item. The computer reads the code, calls up the price, and sends it to the cash register as fast as it takes to make the beeping sound.

The code is twelve digits divided into four numbers. The first number is only one digit and it tells the computer what kind of product it is—cereal or meat or magazine, for example.

The second number is made up of five digits. This is the manufacturer's number, which is assigned by the Uniform Code Council. That number would tell the computer if the item was manufactured by Mattel or Nabisco, for example.

The third number is five digits. That's the product number. It tells the size, color, and other information about the item. It could let the computer know that the customer had bought 1 pound of hotdogs or .875 ounces of ground beef or a pair of tennis socks.

The last digit is the check number that tells the computer if any of the other numbers were wrong. It checks for mistakes.

BEAUFORT'S WIND SCALE

In 1806 a British navy admiral, Sir Francis Beaufort, designed a way to measure the force of the wind. He used a scale from 0 to 12, from the weakest wind to the strongest, which he described as "that which no canvas can withstand." By canvas, he meant the sails on a ship. We use the same basic scale today, but now it has eighteen measurements.

In 1955, the U.S. Weather Bureau added the numbers 13 to 17 to represent different speeds of hurricanes.

Beaufort Number	Wind Speed	Effect on Land	Called
0	less than 1 mph	Smoke rises straight up	Calm
1	1 to 3 mph	Wind blows smoke around	Slight
2	4 to 7 mph	Leaves rustle, feel wind on face	Light breeze
3	8 to 12 mph	Leaves, small branches move	Gentle
4	13 to 18 mph	Wind raises dust/paper	Moderate
5	19 to 24 mph	Small, leafy trees move	Fresh breeze
6	25 to 31 mph	Large branches move	Strong
7	32 to 38 mph	Walking into wind is hard, and large trees move	High wind
8	39 to 46 mph	Twigs break off trees	Gale
9	47 to 54 mph	Slight damage to buildings	Strong gale
10	55 to 63 mph	Trees uprooted, a lot of damage to buildings	Storm
11	64 to 73 mph	Widespread damage	Violent storm
12	74 and up	Devastation, extreme damage	Hurricane

MOHS HARDNESS SCALE

In 1822, a German mineralogist, Friedrich Mohs, made up this scale as a way of comparing the hardness of minerals. Something that measures a 1.0 on the Mohs scale is as soft as talc and can be crushed by a fingernail. A substance on the scale can be scratched by any substance harder than itself on the scale, and it can scratch any one softer than it is. A diamond, for example, can scratch all the other minerals, but the diamond can be scratched only by another diamond.

Mohs Number	Mineral	Hardness Test
1.0	talc	crushed by fingernail
2.0	gypsum	scratched by fingernail
3.0	calcite	scratched by a penny
4.0	fluorspar	scratched by glass
5.0	apatite	scratched by penknife
6.0	feldspar	scratched by quartz
7.0	quartz	scratched by steel file
8.0	topaz	scratched by corundum
9.0	corundum	scratched by diamond
10.0	diamond	scratched by diamond

THE RICHTER SCALE

In 1935, Charles Richter and Beno Gutenburg invented a way to measure the magnitude of an earthquake. The size of the tremors are measured in millimeters on a **seismograph**, and the time between tremors is recorded. The scale goes from 1 to 8. Each level is ten times greater than the one before it. A 7.0 quake is 1,000 times greater than a 4.0 quake, and a quake that measures 8.0 is 10,000,000 times greater than a 1.0 tremor.

MUSICAL SCALES

The word *scale* comes from the Italian word *scala*, meaning step or stairway. There are twenty-four major and minor musical scales. Each scale is a series of eight notes called an *octave*. In some Far Eastern and Oriental countries, there are also twelve-note scales and ten-notes scales.

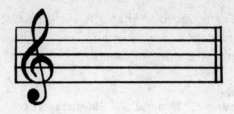

Music is written on five lines and four spaces called the **staff**. The lines represent the pitch.

You can change the pitch a half step up or down by "sharpening" or "flattening" the notes.

♯   sharp   ♭   flat

You can also change the pitch of all the notes to conform to a certain scale. This is done by changing the **key signature** that is found at the left end of the staff.

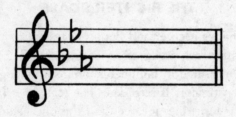

Time signatures look like fractions. They tell you the number of beats in a measure, and the value of each beat. A signature of 4/4 in a measure means that there are four beats in a measure, and the quarter note gets one beat. The top number tells how many beats in a measure, and the bottom number tells the type of note that gets one beat. A 2 means a half note, a 4 means a quarter note, and so on. 3/4 time tells you there are three beats in a measure, and the quarter note gets one beat.

𝅝	whole note		whole rest
𝅗𝅥	half note		half rest
♩	quarter note	𝄽 *or* 𝄾	quarter rest
♪	eighth note	𝄾	eighth rest
♬	sixteenth note	𝄿	sixteenth rest
𝅗𝅥.	dotted half note		dotted half rest

How Many Performers?

- A solo is one person; a soloist performs alone.
- A duet is two.
- A trio has three.
- A quartet has four members.
- A quintet has five.

SYMBOLS ON MAPS AND CHARTS

Weather Maps

Meteorologists are scientists who study the weather. The National Weather Service has 243 offices throughout the country, with 52 forecast stations. Thousands of meteorologists at these stations keep hourly records of changes in temperature, air pres-

Weather Conditions

CLEAR SKY	CLOUDY (PARTLY)	CLOUDY (COMPLETELY OVERCAST)	

DRIZZLE	FOG (LIGHT)	FOG (HEAVY)	HAZE

HURRICANE	LIGHTNING	RAIN SHOWERS	

SANDSTORM OR DUST STORM		HAIL SHOWERS	

SLEET	SNOW	SNOW (DRIFTING, SLIGHT TO MODERATE)

THUNDERSTORM	TORNADO	TROPICAL STORM	VISIBILITY REDUCED BY SMOKE

Wind Speeds

CALM	APPROX. 1 MPH (1 KNOT)	APPROX. 6 MPH (5 KNOTS)	APPROX. 12 MPH (10 KNOTS)	APPROX. 58 MPH (50 KNOTS)

Weather Fronts

WARM	COLD	OCCLUDED	STATIONARY

sure, cloud cover, humidity, and winds. Weather satellites called NIMBUS, LANDSAT, SEASAT, and GEOSAT circle high above the earth, sending back information that is used to prepare the daily forecasts and weather maps. All meteorologists use the same signs and symbols on weather maps.

ROAD MAPS

Every map has a **key** that explains what all the symbols mean.

Map and Chart Symbols

Boundaries

INTERNATIONAL   PROVINCIAL OR STATE   COUNTY   TOWNSHIP   INCORPORATED VILLAGE

Cities and Towns

CAPITAL CITY   URBAN AREA   TOWN OR VILLAGE

Roads and Railroads

SUPERHIGHWAY   SUPERHIGHWAY UNDER CONSTRUCTION   DUAL HIGHWAY   MAIN ROAD   SECONDARY ROAD

BRIDGE AND ROAD   DRAWBRIDGE AND ROAD   TUNNEL AND ROAD   RAILROAD TRACK, SINGLE   RAILROAD TRACKS, TWO OR MORE   RAILROAD STATION

Hydrographic Features

RIVER   INTERMITTENT LAKE   INTERMITTENT RIVER

FRESHWATER LAKE, RESERVOIR   DAMS   FALLS

Natural Features

GLACIERS AND ICE SHELVES   ELEVATION ABOVE SEA LEVEL

PASSES

Interstate Route Markers

Route signs on interstate highways (running between states) mark 42,500 miles of roads that connect 86 percent of the major cities in the United States. The interstate signs are blue shields with red tops and white lettering.

Odd Numbers: Roads that run from north to south are marked with odd numbers. The numbers get larger as they go from west to east, so that a north-south highway in the West might be Route 5, and in the East a major north-south road might be Route 95.

Even Numbers: Roads running east to west use even numbers. Low numbers are used in the South, and higher numbers to the North. In Florida, there is a Route 4, and along the Canadian border, you'll find Route 96.

Zero: Routes from coast to coast end in zero.

Three-Digit: When you see a route number with three digits, you know it's a connecting road or an offshoot of a major route.

U.S. Route Signs

The federal government also marks its roads with odd and even numbers. North-south routes also use odd numbers of one to three digits. Low numbers are used to mark roads in the East. Route 1 would be in the East, and Route 101 in the West.

East-west roads use even numbers; low in the North, high to the South. Route 2 is at the Canadian border, Route 90 at the Rio Grande in Texas.

MILEPOSTS

The little numbers you see on the roadside as you drive by that mark the miles are used by police to locate accidents, and by highway departments to locate signs or places for road repair. A highway patrolman can call for an ambulance at the 16-mile mark, for example.

OCEAN CHARTS

A ship's captain from Belgium and a captain from an American or Canadian freighter can read the same ocean charts. Language isn't a problem when people can read signs and symbols that mean the same thing to everyone. Sea charts show the path of ocean currents, measured in knots. They show the depth of water at low tide and high tide, and the location of lighthouses. Each lighthouse has its own signal, and that is marked on the chart, showing the number of seconds between each flash of light.

Buoys: As a ship goes into a harbor, the odd-numbered buoys are always on the ship's left or port side, and they are painted black. The even-numbered buoys, which are red, are on the ship's right or starboard side. Because the smallest numbers are those farthest out to sea, and the largest numbers are near harbor the captain can tell when he is approaching the harbor. Sailors have an easy way of remembering the buoys; it's three Rs: Red to right, returning.

Starboard and Port: Many years ago, before ships used central rudders at the stern (the back of the ship), ships had a steering oar (or steer) on the right-hand side. That side was called the "board," and after a while it got to be called the starboard side. When a ship pulled into harbor, it tied up on the left side so that the steering oar wouldn't be smashed against the dock. That side then came to be called the port side. All ships underway at night must show a red sidelight to port, a green light to starboard, and a white light on the masthead.

SIGNS, SIGNALS, AND SYMBOLS EVERYWHERE

All around us, signs and symbols are part of our daily lives. We see the flash of right and left turn signals on cars and trucks. The school bus flashes red signals, and all traffic stops. The red, green, and yellow traffic signals need no words to tell drivers what to do. A bell rings in school, and you know it's time for another class or a signal for a fire drill. A skull and crossbones on a bottle tells you it contains poison. A red cross on a box tells you it contains first aid equipment. Referees in basketball, football, and hockey signal scores, touchdowns, penalties, or a dozen other things that all players can "read." Everyone recognizes a baseball umpire's signals for safe, ball, strike, and out.

CATTLE BRANDS

On the open range, cattlemen mark their cattle with a "brand." Each ranch has its own symbol made into a branding iron. The branding iron is heated and the symbols are burned onto the flesh of the cattle. Sometimes they put letters of the alphabet in unusual positions. Lying sideways, they are called "lazy." At an angle, they are called "tumbling."

LAZY S   BAR H   FLYING U   CIRCLE C

Everyday

CHAPTER NINE

Numbers

very day your life is full of numbers. Someone wants to know your zip code, your area code, or your phone number. You go bowling and someone asks what size shoes you wear. A teacher tells you to bring a No. 2 pencil to a test— what's that? This chapter will tell you.

THE MOST IMPORTANT NUMBER

911 is the number you must never forget. It can save your life. In an emergency, 911 will bring help from the police or fire department in most communities. If you are home alone and hurt yourself, or if you think a person is trying to get into your house, or if there is a fire, just dial 911. Give your name and address to the person who answers. And in a calm, clear voice, tell that person why you need help.

In some communities, the 911 number is connected to computers that show the operator the name and address of the person who is calling. If your town has this system, all you have to do is say, "I need help," and you'll get it.

HELPFUL HOTLINES

These phone numbers can connect you with help and information, too. All numbers that start with 800 are called tollfree. That means they are free, even if they are long distance. Remember to dial 1 first: 1-800-then the number.

Youth Crisis and Runaway Hotline

1-800-448-4663. Call any time, night or day.

Drug Abuse Information Line

1-800-522-5353

Child Abuse Reporting Center

1-800-342-3720

Missing Children Hotline (KIDWATCH)

1-800-543-9282. Call any time, night or day.

DO NOT CALL THESE NUMBERS— WITHOUT PERMISSION

900 numbers are advertised on television all the time. They sound exciting because they offer to tell you jokes, let you talk to kids in other states, tell your fortune, or read your horoscope. *Do not call* a 900 number unless your parents have said it's okay, because they *cost a lot of money. One minute* of talking can cost you anywhere from 50 cents to $10.

HOUSE NUMBERS

Napoleon Bonaparte, emperor of France, started the idea of putting odd numbers on houses on one side of the street, and even numbers on the other side. If this is such a sensible idea, how come the odd numbers are on the south or west side of the street in some parts of town, and on the north or east side in other

sections? That happened because towns and cities tend to grow in spurts. Old sections might have used one system, and newer developments another. In the last ten years, planners have been trying to organize cities into one system that will make it easier for the computerized postal system and the 911 emergency services.

SOCIAL SECURITY NUMBER

Every citizen of the United States gets a Social Security number. The first three numbers make up a code for the state you lived in when the number was given to you. Sometimes children get their Social Security number when they are born. If you were born in Memphis, Tennessee, your first three numbers will be between 408 and 415, even if you move to Chicago, Illinois, or Anchorage, Alaska.

The second group of numbers is the code for the year you were given your Social Security card. And the third group of numbers is your own personal number, given at random. ("At random" means you get it by chance. It's like pulling a number out of a hat.)

Your Social Security number will stay with you all your life. It is your identification number that follows you everywhere.

NUMBERS ON ORDINARY EVERYDAY THINGS
Pencils

Have you ever taken the kind of test that was answered by filling in a tiny square with a No. 2 pencil? You read the question on one paper, and fill in a numbered square on an answer sheet with a hard pencil that the test-correcting machine can " read."

The number on the pencil tells how hard or soft it is. Ordinary writing pencils are numbered from 1 to 4. Soft pencils are 1, and the hardest are 4. Pencils used by artists have a different number scale. They range from the softest: 8B, 7B, 6B, 5B, 4B, 3B, 2B, B; to medium-hard: HB, F, H, 2H, 3H, 4H, 5H, 6H, 7H, 8H, 9H; to the hardest, 10H. The thinnest, lightest line can be drawn with the hardest pencil.

- The biggest pencil-user is the United States government. It buys and uses 45 million pencils in one year.
- One pencil can make a line 35 miles long, or write 45,000 words.
- About 300,000 pencils can be made from the average size cedar tree.

Paper

A ream of paper consists of 500 sheets of 8½ by 11 inch paper. But paper is measured in weight. If paper is labeled "20 pound," it means that a stack of 500 sheets of this kind of paper, in sheets measuring 2 feet by 3 feet, weighed in a room at 70 degrees Fahrenheit and 50 percent humidity, will weigh 20 pounds. Newsprint is a fairly flimsy paper used for throwaway things like the daily news. It's made from recycled paper and wood pulp. The sturdiest heaviest paper contains rags and more wood pulp.

Paper Clips

The numbers on paper clips are backward. The bigger number means the smaller paper clip, but no one knows why. There are three sizes: #3, or small; #1, or standard; and jumbo. There is no size number 2.

Rubber Bands

The number on the box of rubber bands tells the size. All sizes numbered from 8 to 19 are ¹⁄₁₆ inch wide. Number 8 is the shortest, and 19 the longest. All rubber bands that are numbered 30 to 39 are ⅛ inch wide. The 30 is shortest, and 39 the longest.

Sunscreen

How do you know what number sunscreen to put on when you go to the beach? The number is called the SPF, for Sun Protection Factor. You have to know how long it takes for your skin to get sunburned, and then you can figure out what sunscreen number you need. If you burn after being in the sun for an hour, you can (according to the sunscreen makers) stay in the sun for five hours if you use a number 5 sunscreen. The higher the number of the sunscreen, the more protection it gives.

Shoe Size

When you walk into a shoe store, a clerk probably asks. "What size do you wear?" Did you know that shoe sizes were originally measured in barleycorns? In the 1300s, grains of barley were laid end to end to measure shoes. If a man's foot measured 39 barleycorns, that was 13 inches. And that was called a size 13. A size twelve was 38 barleycorns, and a 6 was 32 barleycorns. English-speaking nations still use these sizes. The only difference now is that we have right and left shoes, thank goodness. Until 1818, shoes for right and left feet were made the same. Not very comfortable!

Hats

Hats are weird. The most common hat size for a man is 7⅛. The most common size for a woman is 22 inches. Before 1800, mens' hats were made on round wooden forms, in a perfect circle, even though heads are oval. The sizes progressed in eighths of an inch. Most women used to make their own hats at home, or with the help of a dressmaker or milliner (hat maker). They measured around the head with a tape measure.

Socks

No one worries about sock sizes these days. There's "one size fits all," that stretches to fit any foot. But if you do buy socks by size, you'll find a sensible system. If your foot is 10 inches long, you take a size 10 sock. That started in the days before nylon and other stretchy fibers, when socks didn't stretch and didn't stay up. Now there's an even better size, 9–11, which fits sizes 9 and 11, and everything in between.

YOUR PERSONAL IMPORTANT NUMBERS

Keep a record of the numbers that are most important in your life:

Address ___1901 E 3rd___

City or town ___Goldendale___

Zip code ___98620___

Social Security _____

Birthday ___11/3/81___

Phone number Area code ___509___ No. ___773-5394___

Bike combination _____

Locker combination ___15-41-23___

Important phone numbers ___4453-3286-6706-4139-45394___

Funny

CHAPTER TEN

Numbers

A riddle is a kind of guessing game, as old as language itself. One of the oldest is a riddle told thousands of years ago in ancient Greece. A monster known as the Sphinx asked everyone passing by, "What walks on four legs in the morning, two legs at noon, and three legs in the evening?" Those who could not answer were killed. Only Oedipus had the answer. He said it was a man, who crawls on all fours as a baby, walks on two feet when he's grownup, and leans on a cane when he is old.

Here is another very old riddle. The answer is on page 223.

> As I was going to St. Ives
> I met a man with seven wives.
> Each wife had seven sacks.
> Each sack held seven cats.
> Each cat had seven kits.
> Kits, cats, sacks, wives,
> How many were going to St. Ives?

TRY THESE NUMBER RIDDLES

- What has two feet and no legs?
  Answer: 24 inches.
- Mr. Jones is a butcher. He is six feet tall, and his waist measures 40 inches. He wears size 10 shoes. What do you think he weighs?
  Answer: Meat.
- What is "three and two" in baseball?
  Answer: Five, just as anywhere else.
- You bet 25 cents on a football game and the game is called off. What do you get?
  Answer: The quarterback.
- Seven copy cats sat on a fence. One jumped off. How many were left?
  Answer: None.
- A farmer had seventeen sheep. All but nine died. How many did he have left?
  Answer: Nine.
- How long is a piece of string?
  Answer: Twice the distance from the middle to the end.
- Why is it dangerous to do mathematics in the jungle?
  Answer: Because if you add 4 and 4 you get ate!
- What number leaves nothing if you take away half?
  Answer: 8.

- Why is six afraid of seven?
  Answer: Because seven eight (ate) nine.

- What number leaves 3 if you take away half?
  Answer: 8.

- How do you get rid of one?
  Answer: Add G and it's gone.
- Why is a dog with a lame leg like adding 6 and 7?
  Answer: He puts down three and carries one.
- What animal is best at mathematics?
  Answer: Rabbits—they multiply fast.

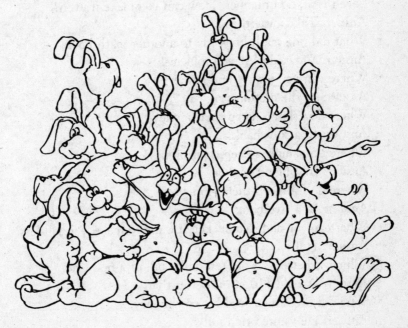

- Why is a school yard larger at recess?
  Answer: Because there are more feet in it.
- Who invented fractions?
  Answer: King Henry the Eighth.
- If I fainted right now, what number would you bring to me?
  Answer: You would bring me 2.
- I have 55 cents, but only two coins. One of them is not a fifty cent piece. What are the two coins?
  Answer: A fifty-cent piece and a nickel. One of them *isn't* a fifty-cent piece, but one of them *is*.
- What occurs once in a minute, twice in a moment, but not at all in a second?
  Answer: The letter *m*.
- What's the best way to double your money?
  Answer: Fold it in half.
- Seven is an odd number. How can you make it even?
  Answer: Take away the *s*.
- What did one math book say to another math book?
  Answer: Wow, do I have problems!
- Where can you always find money?
  Answer: In the dictionary.
- Where do Eskimos keep their money?
  Answer: In a snowbank.
- Where do vampires keep their money?
  Answer: In a blood bank.
- Where do fish keep their money?
  Answer: In a riverbank.
- What can you add to a bucket of water to make it weigh less?
  Answer: Holes.
- Which is better, an old ten dollar bill or a new one?
  Answer: An old $10 bill is better than a $1.
- Why did the farmer feed his cow money?
  Answer: He wanted rich milk.

- When things go wrong, what can you always count on?
  Answer: Your fingers.
- What's the difference between 100 and 1000?
  Answer: Nothing—zero.
- Why did the poor man want to open a pizza shop?
  Answer: He wanted to make some dough.

(*Answer to St. Ives riddle:* Only one person was going to St. Ives.)

A KNOCK KNOCK

Knock Knock.
Who's there?
One two.
One two, who?
Knock knock.
I asked, "Who's there?"
One two.
Well, one two, who?
One too many!

SOME NUMBER PUZZLES

Mixup

Take the numbers 1 to 7 and mix them up in any order. Can
you use each number only once to get 100?
  Answer: $1 + 2 + 34 + 56 + 7 = 100$

On the Line

Can you add five lines to six lines to get nine?

Answer:

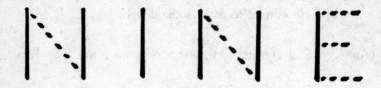

Magic Square

The magic square is one of the oldest number mysteries. More than 3,000 years ago in China it was called Lo Shu. Can you fill in the magic square with the numbers 1 to 9 so that each row adds up to 15 in any direction?

Answer:

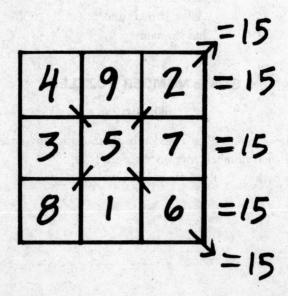

Horses and Stalls

How can you put ten horses in nine stalls, with each horse having its own stall?

Answer:

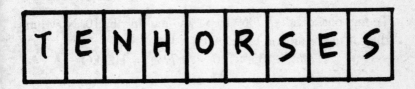

CAN YOUR CALCULATOR SPELL?

Press the numbers 6-6-3. Now turn your calculator upside down. What word do your read? It should say EGG.

- Astound your friends with these words:

BELL (7738)	BIG (618)	BOO (008)
BLOB (8078)	BOIL (7108)	BOSS (5508)
BEG (638)	HOBBIES (5318804)	HELLO (07734)
GOSH (4506)	GLOB (8076)	GOO (006)
HIGH (4614)	HI (14)	HOLE (3704)
LIE (317)	LOSE (3507)	LOOSE (35007)
OIL (710)		SHELL (77345)

What Was Left in the Ocean After the *Exxon Valdez* Ran Aground?

Your calculator can tell you.

Multiply the ship's registration number (4467590) by the captain's lucky number (13). Add the length of the sand bar (40 meters). Now turn your calculator over and you'll have the answer.

$$4467590 \times 13 + 40 = 58078710 \text{ OIL BLOBS.}$$

Is Your Calculator "User Friendly"?

To find out, divide 2.7069 by 35 and multiply by 10. Now turn the calculator around to see what it has to say.

$$2.7069 \div 35 \times 10 = 0.7734 = \text{HELLO}$$

ANOTHER CALCULATOR TRICK

Think of a Number

Practice the trick with several other numbers before you show your friends.

Step 1: Think of a number, for example	14
Step 2: Add 3 to that number	+ 3
	17
Step 3: Double that answer × 2 =	34
Step 4: Subtract 4	− 4
	30
Step 5: Divide that answer in half ÷ 2 =	15
Step 6: Subtract the number you thought of first	−14
Step 7: Your answer should be 1.	1

COUNTING SONGS FOR JUMPING ROPE, CHOOSING SIDES, OR JUST PLAIN FUN

I Caught a Fish

1, 2, 3, 4, 5. Once I caught a fish alive.
6, 7, 8, 9, 10. Then I let him go again.
Why did I let him go?
Cause he bit my finger so.
Which finger did he bite?
The little finger on my right.

One Potato

One potato, two potato, three potato, four,
Five potato, six potato, seven potato more.

Bubble Gum

Bubble gum, bubble gum in a dish,
How many pieces do you wish?
"Five." 1, 2, 3, 4, 5, and out you go.

Number One, Touch Your Tongue

Number one, touch your tongue
Number two, touch your shoe
Number three, touch your knee
Number four, touch the floor
Number five, learn to jive
Number six, pick up sticks
Number seven, go to heaven
Number eight, over the gate

Number nine, touch your spine
Number ten, do it again.

One, Two, Three O'Leary

1, 2, 3, O'Leary
4, 5, 6, O'Leary
7, 8, 9, O'Leary
10, O'Leary caught it.

One, Two, Buckle My Shoe

1, 2, buckle my shoe
3, 4, shut the door
5, 6, pick up sticks
7, 8, lay them straight
9, 10, a big fat hen
11, 12, dig and delve
13, 14, maids a-courting
15, 16, maids in the kitchen
17, 18, maids in waiting
19, 20 that's a plenty.

One Hundred Bottles of Pop on the Wall (some people sing it as bottles of beer on the wall)

One hundred bottles of pop on the wall,
One hundred bottles of pop;
Take one down, pass it around,
Ninety-nine bottles of pop on the wall.
Ninety-nine bottles of pop on the wall,
Ninety-nine bottles of pop,

Take one down, pass it around,
Ninety-eight bottles of pop on the wall.

Keep on singing! You continue counting down to zero, and then start over again!

Here Comes Teacher (for jumping rope)

Here comes teacher with a great big stick.
I wonder what I got in arithmetic.
One, two, three, four, five. . . .

How Old?

I was born in a frying pan.
Can you guess how old I am?
One, two, three, four,
*   five. . . .*

For Heaven's Sake

One, two, three, four, five, six, seven.
All good children go to heaven.
When they get there they will say,
Johnny* went the other way.

(*You put in the name of the kid who is out.)

Bibliography

Adler, David A. *Roman Numerals*. New York: Thomas Y. Crowell, 1977.

Antonacci, Robert J., and Barbara D. Lockhart. *Tennis for Young Champions*. New York: McGraw Hill Book Co., 1982.

Appel, Marty. *The First Book of Baseball*. New York: Crown Publishers, Inc., 1988.

Asimov, Isaac. *Isaac Asimov's Biographical Encyclopedia of Science and Technology*. New Revised Edition. New York: Avon Publishers, 1976.

Becker, Thomas W. *The Coin Makers*. Garden City, N.Y.: Doubleday and Co., 1969.

Bell, Thelma and Corydon. *The Riddle of Time*. New York: Viking Press, 1963.

Bendick, Jeanne. *How Much, How Many*. New York: Franklin Watts, 1989.

Berndt, Fredrick. *The Domino Book*. Nashville, Tenn.: Thomas Nelson Publisher, 1974.

Blocksma, Mary. *Reading the Numbers*. New York: Penguin Books, 1989.

Boehm, David A., editor. *1989–90 Guiness Sports Record Book*. New York: Sterling Publishers, 1989.

Boslough, Stephen. *Hawking's Universe*. New York: William Morrow & Co., 1985.

Bottomley, Tom. *Boatman's Handbook*. New York: Hearst Marine Books, 1985.

Brandneth, Gyles. *Number Play*. New York: Rawson Associates, 1984.

Calder, Nigel. *Timescale. An Atlas of the Fourth Dimension*. New York: Viking Press, 1983.

Campbell, Vice Admiral Gordon, and I. D. Evans. *The Book of Flags*. London: Oxford University Press, 1965.

Coggins, Jack. *Flashes and Flags. The Story of Signaling*. New York: Dodd, Mead, and Co., 1963.

Diagram Group. *Comparisons*. New York: St. Martins Press, 1980.

Dilson, Jesse. *The Abacus: A Pocket Computer*. New York: St. Martins Press, 1968.

Elting, Mary. *Arrow Book of Science Facts*. New York: Scholastic Book Services, 1959.

Emrich, Duncan. *The Hodgepodge Book*. New York: Four Winds Press, 1972.

Freedman, David. "Bolts From the Blue." *Discover*. December 1990.

Forker, Dom. *The Ultimate Baseball Quiz Book*. New York: Signet Books, 1988.

Gallant, Roy. *Man the Measurer*. New York: Doubleday and Co., 1972.

Gardner, Martin. *Relativity for the Millions.* New York: Macmillan Co., 1962.

———. *Archimedes, Mathematician and Inventor.* New York: Macmillan Co., 1965.

Garrison, Webb B. *Why You Say It.* New York: Abingdon Press, 1958.

Goudsmit, Samuel A., Robert Claiborne, and the Editors of Time. *Time.* New York: Time, Inc., 1966.

Grun, Bernard. *The Timetables of History.* New York: Simon and Schuster, Touchstone Books, 1979.

Hammond, Tim. *Sports.* Eyewitness Books. New York: Alfred A. Knopf, 1988.

Harvey, Edmund H. Jr., editor. *Reader's Digest Book of Facts.* Pleasantville, N.Y.: Reader's Digest Association, Inc., 1987.

Hawking, Stephen. *A Brief History of Time.* New York: Bantam Books, 1988.

Hesser, Dalet, and Susan S. Leach. *Focus on Earth Science.* Columbus, Ohio: Merrill Publishing Co., 1987.

Hickok, Ralph. *New Encyclopedia of Sports.* New York: McGraw Hill Book Co., 1977.

Hoffman, Mark, editor. *The World Almanac and Book of Facts 1991.* New York: Pharos Books, 1991.

Hunter, Nigel. *Einstein.* Great Lives Series. New York: Franklin Watts, 1987.

Ireland, Karin. *Albert Einstein.* Pioneers in Change Series. Englewood Cliffs, N.J.: Silver Burdett Press, 1989.

Irwin, Keith. *The 365 Days: The Story of Our Calendar.* New York: Thomas Y. Crowell Co., 1963.

Jaspersohn, William. *Bat, Ball, Glove: The Making of Major League Baseball Gear.* Boston: Little, Brown and Co., 1989.

Johnstone, William D. *For Good Measure.* New York: Avon Books, 1975.

Jones, J. P. *The Money Story.* New York: Drake Publishers Inc., 1973.

Jones, Robert M. *Can Elephants Swim? Unlikely Answers to Improbable Questions.* New York: Time-Life Books, 1969.

Lasne, Sophie, and Andre Gaultier. *A Dictionary of Superstition.* Englewood Cliffs, N.J.: Prentice-Hall, 1984.

Macaulay, David. *The Way Things Work.* Boston: Houghton Mifflin, 1988.

Mallinson, G., J. Mallinson, Smallwood, and Valentino. *Science.* Englewood Cliffs, N.J.: Silver Burdett Co., 1984.

McKenzie, E. C. *Salted Peanuts.* New York: New American Library, Signet Books, 1972.

Meserole, Mike, editor. *The 1990 Information Please Sports Almanac.* Boston: Houghton Mifflin Co., 1989.

Moore, Carl H., and Alvin E. Russell. *Money: Its Origin, Development, and Modern Use.* Jefferson, N.C.: McFarland and Company Publishers, 1987.

Natow, Annette, and Jo-Ann Heslin. *The Cholesterol Counter.* New York: Pocket Books, 1988.

New York Public Library Desk Reference, New York: Webster's New World, 1989.

Nitsche, Roland. *Money.* London: Collins Publishers, 1970.

Opie, Iona, and Moira Tatem. *A Dictionary of Superstitions.* Oxford and New York: Oxford University Press. 1990.

Paton, John, and Leslie Foster, editors. *Mathematics Encyclopedia*. New York: Rand McNally, 1986.

Pennington, Jean A. T. *Food Values*. 15th Revised Edition. New York: Harper and Row Publishers, 1989.

Petersen, Gordon, and A. J. McClintock. *A Guide to Codes and Signals*. Racine, Wisc.: Whitman Publishing Co., 1942.

Potter, Carole. *Knock on Wood*. New York: Beaufort Books, 1983.

Radford, E., and M. A. Radford. *Encyclopedia of Superstition*. New York: Philosophical Library, 1949.

Reisberg, Ken. *Card Games*. New York: Franklin Watts, 1979.

Rochette, Edward. *Making Money*. Fredrich, Colo.: Renaissance House, 1968.

Rosen, Seymour. *Understanding the Human Body*. Biology Workshop 2. New York: Globe Book Company, 1983.

Russ, Alan, editor. *Guiness Book of World Records, 1990*. New York: Sterling Publishing Co., 1990.

Sackson, Sid. *Playing Cards Around the World*. Englewood Cliffs, N.J.: Prentice-Hall, 1981.

Scarne, John. *Scarne's Encyclopedia of Games*. New York: Harper and Row, 1973.

Schwalberg, Carol. *From Cattle to Credit Cards*. New York: Meredith Press, 1969.

Schultz, Pearle and Harry. *Isaac Newton, Scientific Genius*. New York: Garrard Publishers, 1972.

Selfridge, Oliver G. *Fingers Come in Fives*. Boston: Houghton Mifflin, 1966.

Siskin, Bernard, Jerome Staller, and David Rowik. *What Are the Chances?* New York: Crown Publishers, 1989.

Wright, John, editor. *The Universal Almanac.* Kansas City and New York: Andrews and McNeel, 1990.

Index

ILLUSTRATION CREDITS

Illustrations on pages 108, 109, 111, 184, 185, 190, 191, 100 (middle), 201, 202, and 203 are reprinted from *The New York Public Library Desk Reference* © 1989 by the New York Public Library and The Stonesong Press, Inc., by permission of the publisher, Webster's New World/a division of Simon & Schuster.

Illustrations on pages 186–187 are reprinted from *The Boatman's Handbook* courtesy William Morrow & Co.

Illustrations on page 185 are courtesy of the National Information Data Center.